HOW TO SPEAK CELEBRITY

Also by Mitchell Symons

Non-fiction

Forfeit!
The Equation Book of Sports Crosswords
The Equation Book of Movie Crosswords
The *You* Magazine Book of Journolists *(four books, co-author)*
Movielists *(co-author)*
The Sunday Magazine Book of Crosswords
The *Hello!* Magazine Book of Crosswords *(three books)*
How to Be Fat: The Chip and Fry Diet *(co-author)*
The Book of Criminal Records
The Book of Lists
The Book of Celebrity Lists
The Book of Celebrity Sex Lists

The Bill Clinton Joke Book
National Lottery Big Draw 2000 *(co-author)*
That Book
This Book
The Other Book
The Sudoku Institute *(co-author)*
Why Girls Can't Throw
How to Avoid a Wombat's Bum
Where Do Nudists Keep Their Hankies?

Fiction (Headline)

All In
The Lot

HOW TO SPEAK CELEBRITY

Mitchell Symons

headline

First published in Great Britain in 2006 by HEADLINE PUBLISHING GROUP

ISBN 978 0 7553 1575 8

Cataloguing in Publication Data is available from the British Library

Illustrations by Chris Robson
Designed and typeset by The Flying Fish Studios Ltd
Printed and bound in Great Britain by Bath Press

Headline's policy is to use papers that are natural, renewable and recyclable products and made from wood grown in sustainable forests. The logging and manufacturing processes are expected to conform to the environmental regulations of the country of origin.

HEADLINE PUBLISHING GROUP
A division of Hodder Headline
338 Euston Road, London NW1 3BH

www.headline.co.uk www.hodderheadline.com

Contents

Acknowledgements

There are a lot of people who deserve my utmost thanks for helping me compile this book.

First and foremost, I'd like to thank the sublime Andrea Henry of Headline who commissioned this book and also everyone else – especially Val Hudson and Lorraine Jerram – at Headline for looking after me.

I'm extremely grateful to: Chris Tarrant for providing a Foreword; my son Charlie for helping me to select the celebrities, choose/make up the quotes and then annotate them; my indefatigable agent Luigi Bonomi and my infinitely patient and kind wife, Penny. Thanks are also due to Keiran Mellikof and Caroline Bernstein for their uncanny ability to reproduce any voice I requested.

The following also helped – either with the book or (more likely) just by being at the end of a phone with sympathy and cheer when it all got too much for me (ah!): Gilly Adams, Jeremy Beadle, Marcus Berkmann, Jonathan Fingerhut, Jenny Garrison, Richard Littlejohn, Kelvin Mackenzie, William Mulcahy, Nicholas Ridge, Jack Symons, Louise Symons, David Thomas and Rob Woolley.

Mitchell Symons
October 2006
thatbook@mail.com

Introduction

by MITCHELL SYMONS

First of all, an admission. I am not an impressionist. Nor am I a linguist.

But before you curse yourself – or, even worse, curse me – for your folly in buying this book, can I just say that I am a wordsmith and a humorist, not to mention a collector of celebrity trivia, and so this book might be just what you're looking for, after all.

It's fun to do impressions and the aim of this book is to help you imitate your favourite – or, more likely, your least favourite – celebrities: or, to be more accurate, people in the public eye.

I should also say that I'm not a miracle worker. If you have absolutely no ear for voices, then this book will not be able to turn you into an impressionist. Though I would still hope that you could derive enjoyment from the phrases chosen, the way they're treated and also from the trivia.

However, if you've always – perhaps secretly – fancied 'having a go' at a particular person's voice but didn't trust your vocal abilities then, hopefully, the phrases I've chosen, together with the tips on phonetics and pronunciation, and the graphs will give you just enough help to achieve your goal.

At the very least, it will make you appreciate the skill of the professionals.

Because I'm not a linguist, the phonetics I've employed are necessarily – now how can I put this? – amateurish.

But let me defend myself.

If you want to know what real phonetics look like, pick up a dictionary and see how words are treated by real phoneticians. You'll note that it's all absolutely incomprehensible. That's why you're far better off with this phoney phonetician.

Seriously, though, what I've done with my phonetics might not be scientific but I've tried to convey how the words, the voices, the accents and the tones sound to me. Hopefully, that'll work for you, too.

Inevitably, there will be oddities and inconsistencies, but what I've attempted is an impression of phonetics – which is, I hope you'll agree, appropriate enough in a book of impressions.

My elementary system leads to problems that I've found hard to resolve. It's difficult for me to show how, say, Sir Paul McCartney says 'seriously'. The 'us' should be pronounced like the 'ous' in dangerous. There are similar problems with David Bowie's 'bow' and Sir Alex Ferguson's 'grou' (in ground).

However, I feel the advantages of overall simplicity outweigh these few minor quirks. I hope you agree. If you don't, then, in the words of as BSM Williams (as played by Windsor Davies) in *It Ain't Half Hot Mum*: 'Oh dear. How sad. Never mind.' Or, as you'll see later: 'Ooo deeyer. Oww zadd. Nevverr myind.'

I've tried – God knows I've tried – to be eclectic and to include all the major celebrities but I simply couldn't put in people whose voices I couldn't 'hear'.

But there are more than 150 people and characters listed in this book, which leads to some wonderful juxtapositions. I mean, where else are you going to find John Hurt (as Quentin Crisp) alongside Al Pacino (as Michael Corleone) alongside Felicity Kendal (as Barbara Good)?

So, if you don't already own this book and you are thumbing through it in the bookshop, then do yourself a favour and take it home. Making sure, of course, that you pay for it first. After all, you never know who you can do until you do them…

Foreword

by CHRIS TARRANT

Tee hee, Tarrant here!

Well, that's what you'd expect me to say, wouldn't you? After all, it's almost a catchphrase. But the truth is, I have never said it. It was simply how an impressionist once decided to imitate me and that's how every impressionist has 'done' me ever since. Nowadays, I do say 'Tee hee' – but only when I'm imitating people imitating me.

Mitch – the author of the excellent book you're holding – assures me that I'm not alone. He tells me that Humphrey Bogart never said 'Play it again, Sam', that James Cagney never said 'You dirty rat!' and that Captain Kirk never said 'Beam me up, Scottie.' So I am at least in good company.

Looking through the book I see that, for my entry, Mitch has picked 'But we don't want to give you that!' Now I have said that quite a few times, so let me offer you a couple of tips.

In order to look and sound like me, you have to be devastatingly good looking, exceedingly rich and a fine fisherman.

Also, if we ever meet, never assume that you're the first person to say 'But we don't want to give you that', and you certainly won't be the first to say 'Tee hee!'

And if that doesn't tell you everything you need to know about how to do me, I guess Mitch's tips will have to suffice.

Funny People

Ricky Gervais (as David Brent in *The Office*)

'I've created an atmosphere where I'm a friend first and a boss second…Probably an entertainer third.' (Line from the show)

Phonetically: *Aye-eve cree-A-tid an atmuss-feer wair ay-em-er frend furst and-er boss seck-und…proburblee ann enn-er-tay-ner thurd.*

Pronunciation tip: Speak slowly and use your face as much as your voice to recreate the mannerisms.

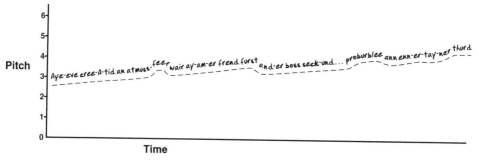

Did you know that Ricky Gervais…?

● sang in a band named Seona Dancing ● is the son of a building labourer ● originally intended to be a marine biologist ● chose Children in Restaurants, Lateness, Children in Need, Caravan Holidays and Noisy People as his *Room 101* choices. Caravan Holidays was the only one that didn't go through

Steve Coogan (as Alan Partridge)

'Back of the net.' (Line from the show)

Phonetically: *Back-ov-ther-nettt.*

Pronounciation tip: Like Coogan himself did, imagine yourself as an Identikit low-grade TV sports reporter. Chew on your words, as though you were trying to dislodge the remains of a Ginster's pie from the roof of your mouth. Sibilate on every 's' sound.

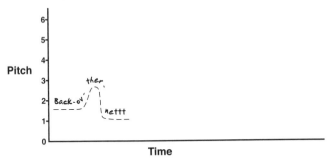

Did you know that Steve Coogan…?
● worked on *Spitting Image* ● won the 1992 Perrier Award at the Edinburgh Festival (*In Character with John Thomson*) ● supports Manchester United

Mike Myers (as Austin Powers)

'Groovy baby.' (Catchphrase)

Phonetically: *Grooo-veee bay-beeee.*

Pronunciation tip: Screw your nose up and make your eyes go all piggy – oh, and get some disgusting teeth. Then ham it up as much as you can. Don't worry about going over the top. Austin doesn't.

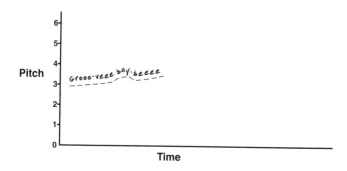

Did you know that Mike Myers…?

- is descended from the poet William Wordsworth ● was the warm-up man for Timmy Mallett
- appeared as a child in an advertisement for Datsun cars ● collects model soldiers

Joan Rivers

'Can we talk?' (Catchphrase)

Phonetically: *Kann wee tawwkk?*

Pronunciation tip: Think Noo York–Brooklyn (pronounced Bervooklyn); a Jewish accent for a voice that's smart, sassy and quick. Use your shoulders and hold nothing back – but don't drive yourself hoarse.

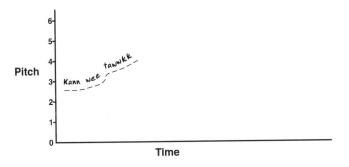

Did you know that Joan Rivers…?
● was born with the name Joan Molinsky ● collects Fabergé eggs ● once said: 'It's been so long since I made love, I can't remember who gets tied up' ● launched a range of her own jewellry

Jonathan Ross

'Round the ragged rocks.' (Imagined phrase)

Phonetically: *Wowund ther wagged wocks.*

Pronunciation tip: Helps if you don't know your rrrrrrrs from your elbow. Also, think cheeky chappie.

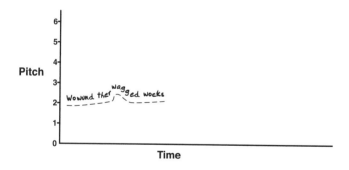

Did you know that Jonathan Ross...?

- appeared as a child in an advertisement for Rice Krispies ● is a keen Scrabble player
- was 21 when he lost his virginity ● collects comics

Eddie Murphy

'Does anyone have a mother that would hit you with a shoe?' (Line from his act)

Phonetically: *Duzzenny-won havver moth-erthartwood hhitt yoo widda shoo?*

Pronunciation tip: Keep your mouth in a fixed rictus grin and think Groucho Marx crossed with a rapper. Also, don't forget the seal-like laugh.

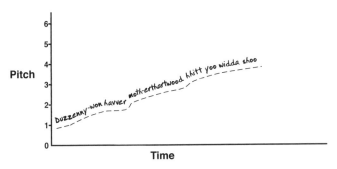

Did you know that Eddie Murphy...?

● swears 262 times in the film *Harlem Nights* ● got his role in *Beverly Hills Cop* after Sylvester Stallone turned it down ● bought the house that was once owned by Cher – 2727 Benedict Canyon Drive ● is the son of a policeman ● was voted Most Popular by his classmates

Matt Lucas (as Daffyd in *Little Britain*)

'I'm the only gay in the village.' (Line from the show)

Phonetically: *Ayim thee own-lee GAY-e inn the villl-edge.*

Pronunciation tip: Welsh – without lapsing, like so many of us do, into Indian. Keep it peevish and precise and lose no opportunity to purse your lips.

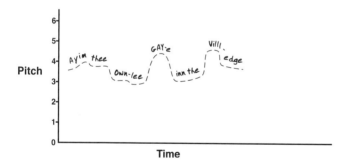

Did you know that Matt Lucas…?

• supports Arsenal • attended the same school as David Baddiel and Sacha Baron Cohen (Haberdashers' Aske's School) • appeared in the video for *Country House* by Blur

David Walliams (as Emily Howard in *Little Britain*)

'I'm a lady.' (Line from the show)

Phonetically: *Eyema LAYDEEE.*

Pronunciation tip: Maximum emphasis on second word. Keep it real: even if you can't be as camp as David Walliams, you can at least attempt verisimilitude.

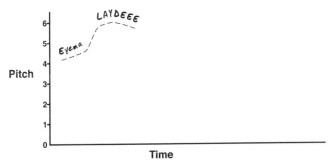

Did you know that David Walliams…?

● was born Williams but he was obliged to change it to Walliams because Equity already had a David Williams
● appeared in the video for *Vindaloo* by Fat Les ● once appeared in *EastEnders* ● met Lucas while both were members of the National Youth Theatre

Eddie Izzard

'Pears can just fuck right off.' (Line from his act)

Phonetically: *Pairz kan juss FUCK rite-off.*

Pronunciation tip: Adopt a surreal, sing-song though quite classy voice while keeping your mouth open at the end of the phrase as though you were trying to catch a passing fly.

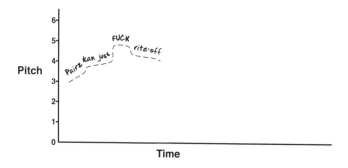

Did you know that Eddie Izzard…?

● was born in Aden – now Yemen ● originally intended to be an accountant ● is partially dyslexic
● is fluent in French and has even performed his show in French

Jackie Mason

'Money is not the most important thing in the world. Love is. Fortunately, I love money.'
(Quote)

Phonetically: *Munn-ee is NUTT derr moest impottant thhing in der world. Luvv iss. Fortoonat-lee, ai luvv munn-eee.*

Pronunciation tip: Cross between Noo York and Mittel European Jewish. Give it lots of (front) tongue. It helps if you keep your shoulders shrugged and disown your words even as you speak them.

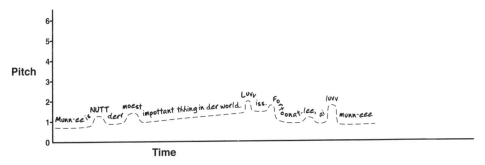

Did you know that Jackie Mason…?

● was born Jacob Maza ● used to be a rabbi – like his father and brothers ● 'appeared' on *The Simpsons* as Rabbi Krustofski

Harry Enfield

'Only me!' (Catchphrase of character known as Mr Don't)

Phonetically: *OOOOAN-LEE MEEE!*

Pronunciation tip: Pitch it high in a light, barking tone and smile as annoyingly as you can.

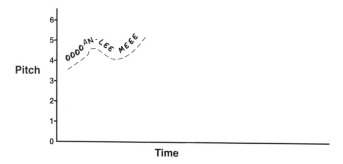

Did you know that Harry Enfield…?

● worked on *Spitting Image* ● had Mark Lamarr as his warm-up man for the *Harry Enfield TV Show*
● chose beer and a cigarette machine as his luxury on *Desert Island Discs*

John Inman (as Mr Humphries in *Are You Being Served?*)

'I'm free!' (Catchphrase)

Phonetically: *Aye-im FREEE!*

Pronunciation tip: As camp as you possibly can – and then some. Makes Dale Winton sound like George Clooney.

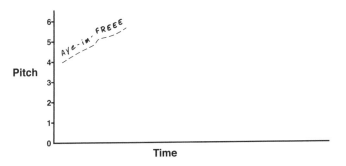

Did you know that John Inman…?

● his character's full name was Wilberforce Clayborne Humphries ● had the codename 'Store' on *This Is Your Life* ● entered into a civil partnership with Ron Lynch, his partner of 33 years, in December 2005

Lenny Henry

'I'd stay away from ecstasy. This is a drug so strong it makes white people think they can dance.' (Line from his act)

Phonetically: *Add stayer-whey fram Ex-ter-see. Thessisa-drugg so strang-et maykes WITE peepul think they-cann danse.*

Pronunciation tip: Pitch your voice between Dudley and urban black America. Go deep from the back of the throat, with plenty of solar plexus.

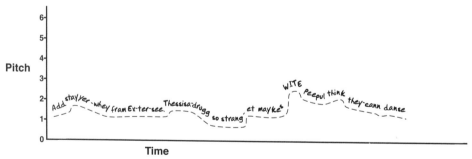

Did you know that Lenny Henry...?

● is a member of the Dennis the Menace Fan Club ● is teetotal ● took an English Literature degree with the Open University ● wrote a children's book called *Charlie and the Big Chill*

Joanna Lumley (as Patsy Stone in *Absolutely Fabulous*)

'Go for it, Eddie.' (Line from the show)

Phonetically: *Goa fr'it-ed-ee.*

Pronunciation tip: Drawl in a lazy, upper-class accent rather than speak. Say every word as though you were resenting the fact that you couldn't talk and drink Champagne at the same time. Keep it quite nasal. Smoking a cigarette helps.

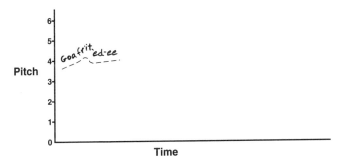

Did you know that Joanna Lumley…?

● was a convent schoolgirl ● was married for only four months to Jeremy Lloyd ● had a rose named after her
● is a patron of Pipedown, the campaign against piped music

Frankie Howerd

Oooh, no missus.' (Catchphrase)

Phonetically: *Oooooowa noo misssis.*

Pronunciation tip: Purse your lips, keep your back teeth closed and try speaking through your nose. Think very camp and say it as though you're simultaneously intrigued and appalled.

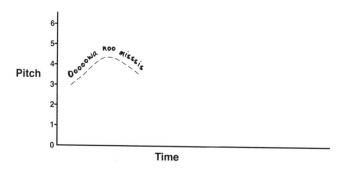

Did you know that Frankie Howerd...?

● overcame a stammer ● failed an audition for RADA ● suffered a nervous breakdown at the start of the 1960s ● died on 19 April 1992 – the day before Benny Hill died

Billy Connolly

'There are two seasons in Scotland – Winter and July.' (Quote)

Phonetically: *Therra TAE seezuns-in Skortlund – Wunterr-and Jilli.*

Pronunciation tip: Standard Glaswegian – surprisingly untouched by the years spent in lalaland – with added music and great vigour. For the full effect, point your bottom out as you speak.

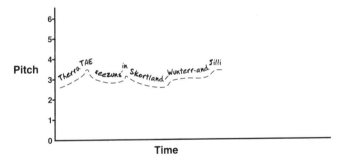

Did you know that Billy Connolly…?

● topped a survey to find Britain's top fantasy cab companion ● grew up in poverty and was a teenage runaway ● has pierced nipples ● is a practising Buddhist

Graham Norton

'No, don't.' (Imagined phrase)

Phonetically: *Nyoo, deeyoant.*

Pronunciation tip: Camp as you can – but knowingly and deliberately so. Chew the words just as they're escaping your lips.

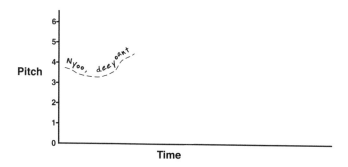

Did you know that Graham Norton...?

● used to be a waiter ● was stabbed in the chest by muggers who left him for dead ● appeared as himself in *Brookside* ● won the 2000 Male Rear of the Year award

John Cleese (as Basil Fawlty in *Fawlty Towers*)

'You'll have to forgive him. He's from Barcelona.'

Phonetically: *Yawull haff too foorgiv him. Heyis from bar-sir-loana.*

Pronunciation tip: What can I tell you about Basil Fawlty that you don't already know? Repressed, depressed, snobbish middle-class Englishman who knows his place and wishes everyone else knew theirs. So keep your tone clipped and steady – even though you're only just managing to keep it all together.

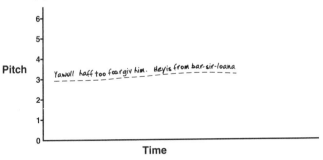

Did you know that John Cleese...?

● bought Bryan Ferry's Holland Park house in 1977 (for £80,000). He sold it in 2001 for £5 million
● didn't lose his virginity until he was in his twenties ● chose a life-sized papier-mâché model of Margaret Thatcher and a baseball bat as his luxury on *Desert Island Discs* ● was Rector of St Andrews University 1970–73

Andrew Sachs (as Manuel in *Fawlty Towers*)

'Mr Fawlty, please understand. If he go, I go.' (Line from the show where Manuel is trying to keep his pet rat)

Phonetically: *Meesturr Foal-tee, poliss unda-stan. Figo, eyego.*

Pronunciation tip: Cartoon Spanish accent, not necessarily from Barcelona. Best done by someone who has German as their first language.

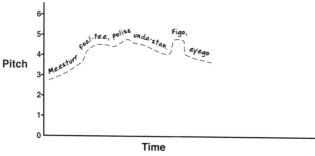

Did you know that Andrew Sachs...?

● was born in Germany but fled to escape Nazi persecution ● was almost knocked out with a heavy saucepan by John Cleese during a recording of the show: Sachs had a two-day headache ● has presented the TV show *Points of View*

Jasper Carrott

'Laughter is the best medicine – unless you're diabetic, then insulin comes pretty high on the list.' (Quote)

Phonetically: *Laffter-iss thur best med-sinn unn-less yoor die-a-bet-ick then ince-ewelin cumms prittee hiyon thurlisst.*

Pronunciation tip: Sing-song blokey Brummie accent which you can achieve by sucking in your cheeks and letting as much of the sound as possible come through your nose.

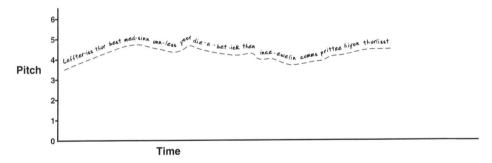

Did you know that Jasper Carrott…?

● was born Robert Davies ● was a Butlin's Redcoat ● was a director of Birmingham City FC (1979–82)
● is the father of Lucy Davis, who played Dawn in *The Office*

Julian Clary

'The English like eccentrics. They just don't like them living next door.' (Quote)

Phonetically: *Thee ing-lish liyek ex-senn-trix. They just doant liyek them livv-ing next door.*

Pronunciation tip: Obviously Quentin Crisp never had a son but if he had…Camp – obviously – but also take care to savour your words and load them with knowing and innuendo.

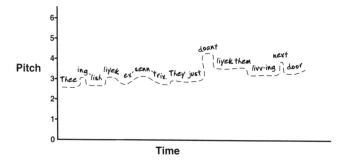

Did you know that Julian Clary…?

● has had Botox treatment ● worked as a singing telegram ● presented *Top of the Pops* ● has suffered from agoraphobia ● is the son of a policeman

Ben Elton

'Yes indeed.' (Catchphrase)

Phonetically: *Yess-inn-DEEEYD.*

Pronunciation tip: A cross between Alan Partridge and Johnny Vaughan – taken down a social class or two. If I were describing a wine, I would also claim that there were 'notes' of other people, too (the Reverend Ian Paisley and Max Miller).

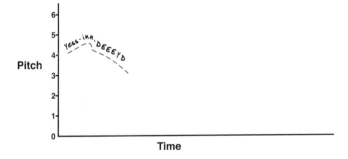

Did you know that Ben Elton...?

● worked on *Spitting Image* ● has always refused to do commercials ● is the father of twins

Woody Allen

'Money is better than poverty, if only for financial reasons.' (Quote)

Phonetically: *Munnee-yis BETT-er thayn pov-errtee iff-ownlee foor fiNAN-shull reesuns.*

Pronunciation tip: Whiny, educated New (as opposed to Noo) York Jew. For the full effect, use your shoulders, hands and arms as much as you can but open your (lower) mouth to its utmost extent when you're looking to be emphatic.

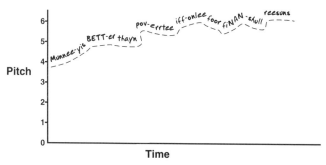

Did you know that Woody Allen…?

● eats out every day of the year ● won't take a shower if the drain is in the middle ● has suffered from Obsessive Compulsive Disorder (OCD) ● was bullied at school because of his name: Allen Konigsberg. 'I'd tell them my name was Frank but they'd still beat me up.'

Windsor Davies (as BSM Williams in *It Ain't Half Hot Mum*)

'Oh dear. How sad. Never mind.' (Catchphrase)

Phonetically: *Ooo deeyer. Oww zadd. Nevverr myind.*

Pronunciation tip: Stomach in, chest out and speak from deep inside your diaphragm. It helps if you're Welsh, male, moustachioed and a non-commissioned Army officer (*lovely boys*).

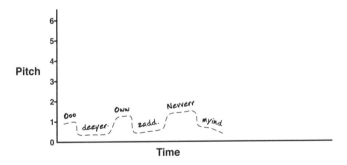

Did you know that Windsor Davies…?

● was a teacher and a miner before becoming an actor ● supports Crystal Palace ● had a Number One hit, *Whispering Grass*, with Don Estelle (Lofty in *It Ain't Half Hot Mum*)

Wilfrid Brambell (as Albert in *Steptoe and Son*)

'Don't leave me, Harold.' (Line from the show)

Phonetically: *Dowunt leeve mee, arr-old.*

Pronunciation tip: Brambell's real voice was, in fact, very posh. As Albert, he found an unappealing voice that was common, grating and alternately plaintive and aggressive in tone. To produce and then maintain the effect, he kept his face permanently screwed up in a leer that made him look like the winner of a gurning contest who hadn't been able to return to normal when it was over.

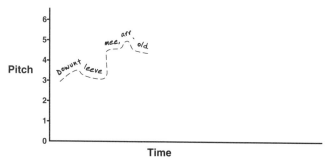

Did you know that Wilfrid Brambell...?

● played Paul McCartney's (fictional) grandfather in *A Hard Day's Night* ● was only 13 years older than Corbett ● was bisexual ● appeared in the 1935 original version of *The 39 Steps*

Harry H. Corbett (as Harold in *Steptoe and Son*)

'You dirty old man!' (Catchphrase)

Phonetically: *Ewe DERRR-TEE OWALD mann!*

Pronunciation tip: Harold had pretensions/delusions of grandeur and affected to despise his common – in every sense of the word – father, whose disgusting behaviour always gave him ample opportunity to trot out his favourite reproach. Deliver it with maximum disgust and despair.

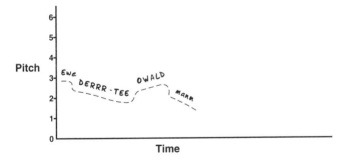

Did you know that Harry H. Corbett…?

- added the 'H' (which he said stood for 'Hanyfing') to avoid confusion with Sooty's handler Harry Corbett
- was married to the actress Sheila Steafel ● served in the Marines during World War II

Peter Kay

'*Bull*seye weren't like any other programme I watched, as it were crap and it were good at same time.' (Line from his act)

Phonetically: *BOULL-zeye wunt lar-kenny uth-errr PROO-grum ah wotch'd azitwer CRAPP anditwer GOODE att'seame tiyim.*

Pronunciation tip: Peter Kay is from Bolton and the great thing about the Bolton accent is that you can get a fix on it simply by saying the word 'Bolton' *(balll-ttun)*. Otherwise, clench your teeth, let your lips go completely and let the words flop out.

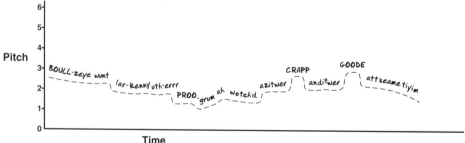

Did you know that Peter Kay...?

● had Steve Coogan's father as his metalwork teacher ● became teetotal after seeing his father die from the effects of alcoholism ● was the warm-up man for *Parkinson*

Bernard Manning

'If you want a good laugh, come and see your Uncle Bernard.' (Quote)

Phonetically: *Effyerwontergoodlaff cumenseeyerun-kel Burrnudd.*

Pronunciation tip: Thick, old Mancunian – and that's just the accent. He says everything in a single breath and speaks as though he's just about to have a heart attack. So should you. Putting on several stones and developing an insensitivity to other races and cultures would help the impression but possibly hinder you in other areas of your life.

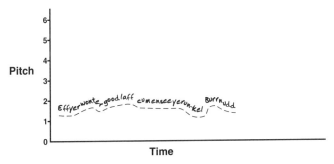

Did you know that Bernard Manning...?

● was a church altar boy ● did his National Service in the Military Police and one of his duties was guarding Albert Speer and Rudolf Hess in Spandau ● bought the numberplate BJM LAF1 ● is teetotal

Paul Whitehouse (as Rowley Birkin QC)

'I was very very drunk.' (Catchphrase)

'**Phonetically:** *Eye wozh vey VVEY drun-ke.*

Pronunciation tip: Being drunk would be a help, but this is easy to do so long as you remember to slur and mutter in equal proportion.

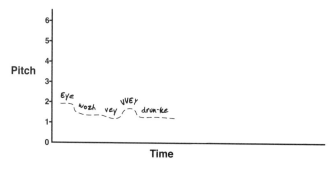

Did you know that Paul Whitehouse…?

● won the Baby Smile of the Rhondda Valley award in 1963 ● shared a flat with Harry Enfield with whom he created the character Loadsamoney ● appeared with his two daughters in the film *Finding Neverland*, alongside his friend Johnny Depp

Tony Hancock

'Stone me, what a life.' (Catchphrase)

Phonetically: *StOAn mee, watta lie-ef.*

Pronunciation tip: Raise your nose while depressing your lower jaw. Think and look lugubrious and put upon.

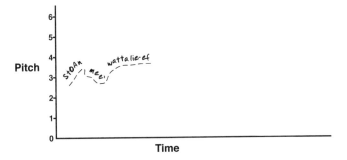

Did you know that Tony Hancock…?

● had a father who ran a small hotel, but was also a comedian and entertainer ● committed suicide in Australia in 1968 at the age of 44. In his suicide note he wrote, 'Things just went wrong too many times'

Sacha Baron Cohen (as Ali G)

'Is it because I is black?' (Catchphrase)

Phonetically: *Iz-itt bee-coz eyeiz blaack?*

Pronunciation tip: This is as complicated as it gets. Basically, you have to try to be a middle-class Jewish boy from North West London who's trying to be a black/Asian working-class youth with the intertext that it's all meant to be an ironic, post-modern satire on people's desire to be simultaneously hip and unwilling to offend other cultures. Good luck.

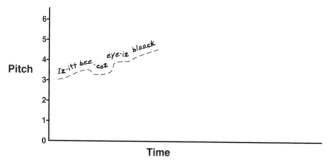

Did you know that Sacha Baron Cohen…?

● is the son of a menswear shop owner ● attended the same school as Matt Lucas and David Baddiel (Haberdashers' Aske's) ● was in the Cambridge University Footlights

Rik Mayall (as Rick in *The Young Ones*)

'We never clean the toilet, Neil. That's what being a student is all about. No way, Harpic; no way, Dot.'

Phonetically: *We NEVERR cleen ve toylett, neel. VAT's watt bee-ink a stewdan-tiz wall-about. No WEAY, HAARpick; no WEAY, DOTT.*

Pronunciation tip: Said sneeringly and with oodles of (misplaced) righteous self-confidence. Screw up your nose and buck your teeth. Helps if you're a comic genius and/or wearing a yellow boilersuit.

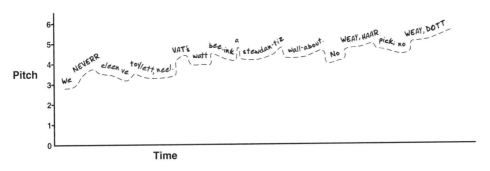

Did you know that Rik Mayall...?

● shared a flat with Rowland Rivron ● is the son of two drama teachers ● made a guest appearance in *The Bill*

Groucho Marx

'I never forget a face but in your case I'll make an exception.' (Quote)

Phonetically: *I nearva fagetta face buddin yaw case, al mayke an ix-sep-shoon.*

Pronunciation tip: Grin as widely as you can without actually smiling and move your lips as little as possible.

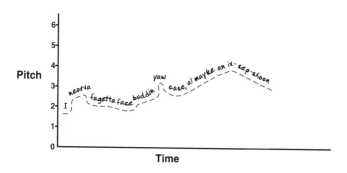

Did you know that Groucho Marx...?

● ate his first bagel at the age of 81 ● shoplifted as a child ● suffered from insomnia ● lost his virginity to a prostitute ● had his appendix removed

Kenneth Williams

'Oh, don't be like that.' (Catchphrase)

Phonetically: *O, doah bee lyyy-ek thaaht.*

Pronunciation tip: Kenneth Williams had several different stock voices – including the one that came from the back of his throat and sounded as if his adenoids were being pulled out by a torturer. The voice required for the line above was camper, more common and more frivolous. Screw up your nose and tighten your eyes and emit a low hum while you say it.

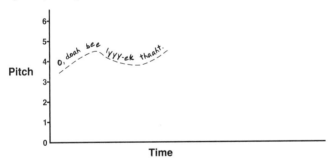

Did you know that Kenneth Williams…?

● provided voices for the PG Tips chimps ● was the son of a barber whom he didn't like ● originally trained as a draughtsman ● proposed a celibate marriage to Joan Sims but she turned him down

Tommy Cooper

'Just like that.' (Catchphrase)

Phonetically: *Jess la tha.*

Pronunciation tip: Spread your hands while you say it – jess la (sorry, just like) Tommy himself. However, the best tip is to say just do the standard Tommy Cooper impersonation – beloved of second-rate TV impersonators right the way through the 1970s. Sorry not to be more original but don't blame me, blame all those 1970s second-rate TV impersonators.

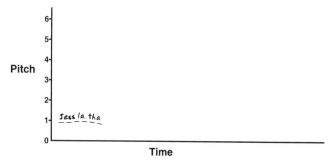

Did you know that Tommy Cooper...?

- died on stage ● was 6' 4" tall ● was a fine magician and only pretended to get things wrong
- was an extremely heavy drinker

Homer Simpson

'Son, you don't want beer. That's for daddies and kids with fake IDs.' (Line from the show)

Phonetically: *Saun, yew dohnt wohnt beeeeer. Thasst fur daddees and kidz with fayek eyedeeez.*

Pronunciation tip: Lift your cheekbones and keep them high. If you watch Dan Castellaneta, you'll notice that he rarely moves his lips when he does Homer.

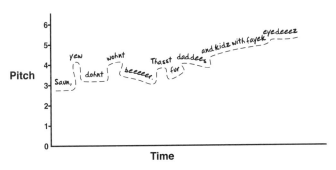

Did you know that Homer Simpson…?

● started out as an imitation of Walter Matthau, but Castellaneta had trouble with certain intonations, so he slightly changed the voice of Homer at the beginning of the second season of the show ● Homer's favourite word – 'd'oh' – appears only as 'Annoyed Grunt' in *Simpsons* scripts

Marge Simpson

'He calls out his bowling ball's name during sex.' (Line about Homer, from the show)

Phonetically: *Hee kawls owt his bOAWALLing baawls nayim jure-ing sechs.*

Pronunciation tip: Grate your voice and go as high pitched as possible. Try adding Marge's trademark grunt – you know, that one that goes 'Hmmm' in a really high-pitched way.

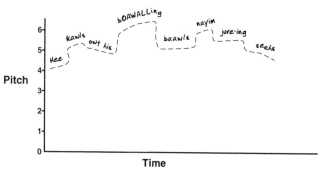

Did you know that Marge Simpson…?

● has pulled a pencil, a huge jar of cash, a cat, a dummy for Maggie and a beach umbrella out of her hair
● has had jobs including police officer, estate agent, professional artist, teacher, novelist, waitress and bodybuilder ● likes buttered noodles, julienned potatoes and peach crumble

Ned Flanders

'Okilly-dokilly.' (Catchphrase)

Phonetically: *Aukillee-dockillee.*

Pronunciation tip: Because Ned uses non-words, there's very little difference between what and how he says things. So repeat them in as earnest a Northern American voice as you can, with just a *soupçon* of surprise. Think William H. Macy in *Boogie Nights* or, indeed, any other film he's ever been in.

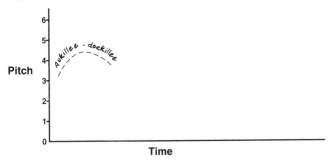

Did you know that Ned Flanders…?

● lost his wife Maude in a NASCAR accident ● owns the Leftorium, a shop selling left-handed products
● is a scoutmaster ● is voiced by Harry Shearer, who was, of course, a member of the seminal heavymetal band, Spinal Tap

Mr Burns

'What good is money if it can't inspire terror in your fellow man?' (Line from the show)

Phonetically: *Wutt good is mun-ee if it carnt in-spy-er terrorin yawr fell-o man?*

Pronunciation tip: Pronounce all the consonants clearly and talk in a feeble, old way. Think Vincent Price's weedier brother.

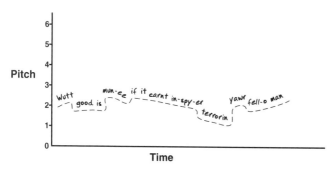

Did you know that Mr Burns...?

● has the full name Charles Montgomery Burns, a riff on Charles Foster Kane in *Citizen Kane*
● is very old indeed and claims to have known President Calvin Coolidge, who left office in 1929
● once tried to buy Cuba ● lives at 1000 Mammon Street

Actors and Actresses

Sir Sean Connery (as James Bond)

'My name's Bond, James Bond.' (Catchphrase)

Phonetically: *My naimsh Barnd, Jaimsshe Barnd.*

Pronunciation tip: Just imitate everyone else's imitation, because that's what they all do, but try not to overdo the lisp. He is, after all, Sean Connery and not Bonnie Langford doing Violet Elizabeth Bott in *Just William*.

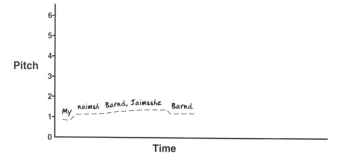

Did you know that Sir Sean Connery…?

● is the son of a lorry driver ● used to work as a French polisher ● appeared in a party political broadcast for the Scottish Nationalist Party ● composed a ballet (*Black Lake*) ● was in the Navy

Arnold Schwarzenegger

'I'll be back.' (Line from *The Terminator*)

Phonetically: *Al be beck.*

Pronunciation tip: Growl the words as though you had German as a first and second language. Bit like Arnie, in fact.

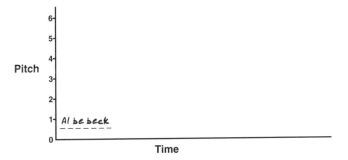

Did you know that Arnie…?

● bought an Army tank ● has a heart murmur ● not only was a bodybuilding champion but also won the Austrian Junior Olympic Weightlifting Championship ● was featured on a stamp in Mali

John Hurt (as Quentin Crisp in *The Naked Civil Servant*)

'Any film, even the worst, is better than real life.' (Line from the film)

Phonetically: *ENN-ee phillm EE-venn ther WURR-st iss BETT-er than REE-ull lie-fe.*

Pronunciation tip: Do your deepest, most gravelly voice and then try to take it as high as you can within that range.

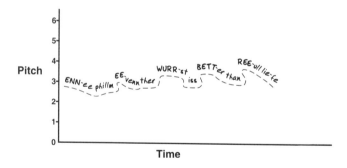

Did you know that John Hurt…?

● is the son of a clergyman ● is a member of the MCC ● trained to be a painter at Grimsby Art School
● has a brother who became a monk

Samuel L. Jackson (as Jules Winnfield in *Pulp Fiction*)

'And I will strike down upon thee with great vengeance...' (Line from the film)

Phonetically: *Eend-aah wil STTR-EYE-EK dowen apowen theee with GRAYET ven-gentss...*

Pronunciation tip: Think like a hellfire preacher: roar like a lion. Hold nothing back.

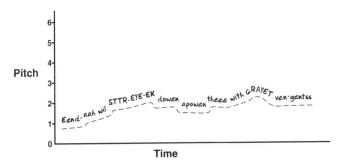

Did you know that Samuel L. Jackson...?

● was Bill Cosby's stand-in for three years on *The Cosby Show* ● overcame a stammer ● can play the French horn and trumpet

Al Pacino (as Michael Corleone in *The Godfather: Part II*)

'I know it was you, Fredo. You broke my heart. You broke my heart!'

Phonetically: *Eye KNOW-it wuzz-yo Fray-do. Yo brock my hart. Yo BROCK my harrt!*

Pronunciation tip: A combination of 1930s Jimmy Cagney, 1950s James Stewart and 1970s Dustin Hoffman. The best way to achieve this voice is to think of yourself as a talking Morse code operator with sandpaper in your larynx.

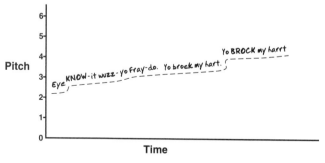

Did you know that Al Pacino...?

● got his breakthrough role as Michael Corleone only after Warren Beatty turned it down ● has turned down plenty of roles – most notably Richard Gere's role in *Pretty Woman* and Harrison Ford's role in *Star Wars* ● started out as a stand-up comic ● does yoga ● is a keen chess player

Alan Bennett

'I don't know.' (Quote)

Phonetically: *Ay chjoant gnoooooo.*

Pronunciation tip: These three words are definitely your best way in to Alan Bennett's unique voice which is a mixture of Yorkshire, scholarly, clerical and camp in a sing-song tone.

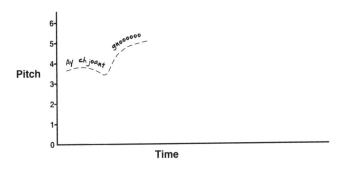

Did you know that Alan Bennett…?
● is the son of a butcher ● recovered from cancer of the colon ● turned down a knighthood

Sylvester Stallone (as John Rambo)

'Mission accomplished.' (Line from *Rambo: First Blood Part II*)

Phonetically: *Mieeszen er-comm-plisht.*

Pronunciation tip: Before saying anything in a Sly Stallone voice, clear your voice – as he does – by intoning 'dah weear' like a constipated primate. Force the sound through your nose, don't forget the lisp and try to make your voice sound as though you've been recorded and played backwards and then replayed forwards.

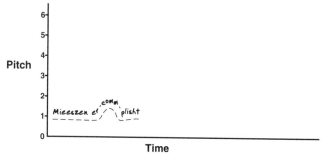

Did you know that Sylvester Stallone…?

● uses his middle name as a first name. He was born Michael Sylvester Stallone ● named two of his children Sage Moonblood and Sistine Rose ● was voted by his classmates Most Likely to End Up in the Electric Chair ● worked as a lion-cage cleaner ● named his dog Gangster

Dustin Hoffman (as Benjamin Braddock in *The Graduate*)

'Mrs Robinson, you're trying to seduce me.' (Line from the film)

Phonetically: *Muisses RARB-in-sunn yerr tri-ing too sed-ooce mee.*

Pronunciation tip: Incredibly nasal with all intonation coming as a surprise to the speaker.

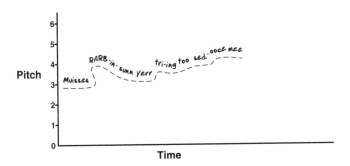

Did you know that Dustin Hoffman…?

● originally intended to be a concert pianist ● only got his big break in *The Graduate* after Robert Redford turned down the part ● lost his virginity with a girl who thought he was his older brother ● lost the tip of his finger when a seat collapsed while filming *Finding Neverland* in 2003

Barbara Windsor (as Peggy Mitchell in *EastEnders*)

'Get out of my pub.' (Line from the show)

Phonetically: *Geht ow'er mah pab.*

Pronunciation tip: Have your mouth wide open while you speak and push your upper lip towards your nose.

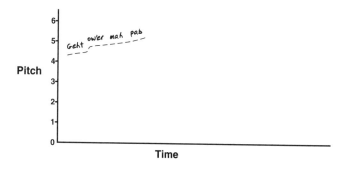

Did you know that Barbara Windsor…?

● is the daughter of a bus driver ● won the 1976 Rear of the Year award ● turned down advances from Warren Beatty ● was a convent schoolgirl

Renée Zellweger (as Bridget Jones)

'Wait a minute…nice boys don't kiss like that.' (Line from Bridget Jones's Diary)

Phonetically: *Whaita min-it…naice boys don't kislaik thatt.*

Pronunciation tip: More British than British. Home Counties with just a trace of Estuary and urban London. Push your lips out and pull your neck back to get the full effect.

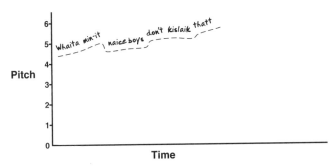

Did you know that Renée Zellweger…?

● keeps a 'grateful journal', a collection of her favourite things, on her bedside table ● worked as a waitress in a topless bar – although she refused to take off her bra ● is fluent in German ● was married to Kenny Chesney for just four months ● was a star cheerleader

Clint Eastwood

'…you've got to ask yourself a question: Do I feel lucky? Well, do you, punk?' (Line from *Dirty Harry*)

Phonetically: *You gotta ass yerself a kwestyan: do I feeel luckee? Well, doo ya, ppunk?*

Pronunciation tip: Keep your teeth gritted the whole time.

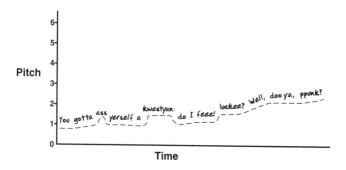

Did you know that Clint Eastwood…?

● made his name as the Man With No Name in a series of Spaghetti Westerns and yet he's allergic to horses ● lost his virginity at the age of 14 – with a 'friendly neighbour' ● survived a plane crash ● once said, 'I've never considered myself addicted to anything, but if I was, sex was it'

Dame Maggie Smith

'One went to school, one wanted to act, one started to act, and one's still acting.' (Quote)

Phonetically: *Won wentt too skooool, won wonted too acctt, won started too acctt, andd wons still acting.*

Pronunciation tip: Pronounce each word as clearly as possible – making the most of every syllable. Use your mouth as much as you can and keep the breathing as even as possible.

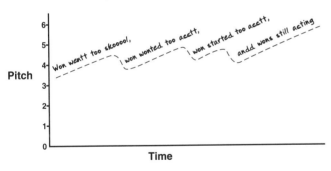

Did you know that Maggie Smith...?

● has been awarded honorary university doctorates by London University, St Andrews and Cambridge
● is the only actress to win an Oscar for playing an Oscar nominee (*California Suite*) ● is the mother of the actor Toby Stephens

Humphrey Bogart

'Louis, I think this is the beginning of a beautiful friendship.' (Last line of *Casablanca*)

Phonetically: *Loo-ee, eye thenk this-iz ther berginning-ov-er bee-yooteefull frand-shipp.*

Pronunciation tip: Speak quizzically, holding your head to one side and lifting your uppermost cheek. Don't forget the trademark drawl and lisp – although you can forego getting the top of your upper lip damaged to get it absolutely right. There's humour and world-weariness there too.

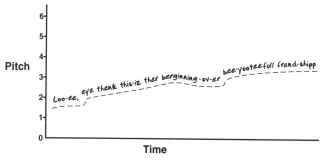

Did you know that Humphrey Bogart…?

● was the son of a doctor ● was expelled from Phillips Academy ● was 45 when he met the 19-year-old Lauren Bacall. She became his fourth wife ● was buried with a whistle in his coffin, placed there by Bacall in memory of her famous line in *To Have and Have Not*

Tony Curtis (pretending to be Cary Grant in *Some Like It Hot*)

'The ship is in ship-shape shape.' (Line from the film)

Phonetically: *Der ship-iz inn ship-shaype shaype.*

Pronunciation tip: Basically, like Curtis does in the film, you're doing a larger-than-life impersonation of Grant so warm up for it by saying 'Judy, Judy, Judy' in a Grant accent – which was the way impressionists always 'did' Grant, even though Grant himself never said those words.

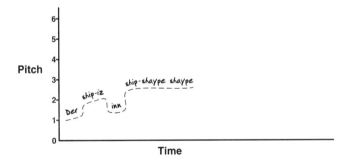

Did you know that Tony Curtis...?

● was born with the name Bernard Schwartz ● served in the US Navy in the Pacific where he witnessed the Japanese surrender ● was on the cover of *Sgt. Pepper's Lonely Hearts Club Band* ● has married five times

Hugh Grant (as Charles in *Four Weddings and a Funeral*)

'Ehm, look. Sorry, sorry. I just, ehm, well, this is a very stupid question and…' (Line from the film)

Phonetically: *Emm, lookk. Sorr-ee, sorree. Yi justt emm, well, this-issa verr-ee stewpid kwest-yun-andd…*

Pronunciation tip: Charles is an upper-middle-class Englishman – a part Grant has played in more than a few films – who, like so many of his ilk, is simultaneously supremely confident and yet totally embarrassed by his own very existence. Solve that paradox and you're halfway to succeeding in this impression. The floppy fringe and the dashing good looks are a bonus.

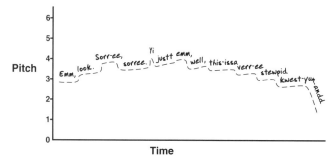

Did you know that Hugh Grant…?

● endowed a scholarship at his old school (Latymer Upper in West London) ● has the middle name Mungo
● worked in advertising as an account executive ● has a single-figure golf handicap

James Gandolfini (as Tony Soprano in *The Sopranos*)

'I'm like King Midas in reverse. Everything I touch turns to shit.' (Line from the show)

Phonetically: *Yeyim laik king my-dass-in ree-versse. Evreething-eye tutch turnz too schitt.*

Pronunciation tip: Perfect cross between Bruce Springsteen and Robert De Niro in *Goodfellas* – with just a little lisp added on every 't'. But don't tell Tony I said that.

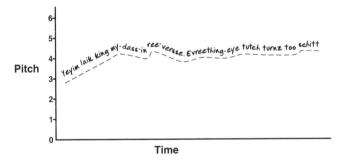

Pitch / Time

Did you know that James Gandolfini…?

● plays the trumpet and saxophone ● used to be a bartender and a bouncer ● was voted Best Looking by his classmates

Leslie Phillips

'Ding dong!' (Catchphrase)

Phonetically: *Dinggg donggg!*

Pronunciation tip: Upper-class chap who's just on the right side of being a bounder – well, that was the character that the hugely underrated Phillips played in so many films. Never forget that comedy is harder than tragedy. You might want to warm up for this by saying 'I say!'

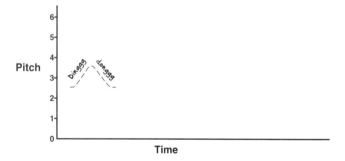

Did you know that Leslie Phillips...?

● recovered from a nervous breakdown ● married Angela Scoular, a former Bond girl ● holds an OBE
● is a Tottenham Hotspur supporter

Jack Nicholson

'My best feature's my smile. And smiles – pray heaven – don't get fat.' (Quote)

Phonetically: *Myy best fee-cherrs-my smy-al yand smy-all-s pray hevv-an doant geht fatt.*

Pronunciation tip: Raise your cheekbones and widen your eyes (preferably behind shades) and keep your teeth fairly gritted. Jack's pronunciation is pretty much the same in all his films – just add or subtract menace, humour, anger, geniality, irritation, etc. Avoid sibilance, however.

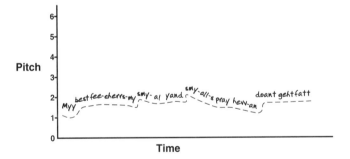

Did you know that Jack Nicholson...?

● had a mother who, as far as the rest of the world was concerned, was his 'sister' ● co-wrote *Head* – the only film The Monkees ever made ● was in detention every day for a whole school year ● is an atheist

Morgan Freeman (as Red in *The Shawshank Redemption*)

'Prison life consists of routine, and then more routine.' (Line from the film)

Phonetically: *Prizz-en liyef conSISts-ov rooteen and theyn moor rooteen.*

Pronunciation tip: Keep your tone rich, deep and even. Don't try too hard, though it's inevitable that you will as it's really difficult to achieve that great sound effortlessly. Less is more. Imagine you're talking with a voice full of top-grade honey.

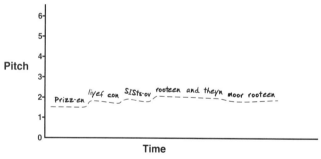

Did you know that Morgan Freeman…?

● trained as a ballet dancer ● started out in the soap opera *Another World* ● named his daughter Morgana
● originally intended to be a fighter pilot

Ricky Tomlinson (as Jim Royle in *The Royle Family*)

'My arse.' (Catchphrase)

Phonetically: *Myy EARRSSE.*

Pronunciation tip: Working-class Scouse. Need I say more?

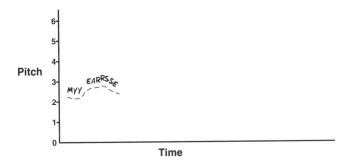

Did you know that Ricky Tomlinson…?

● went to jail for two years in 1972 for conspiracy to intimidate other builders during picket-line violence
● was once a member of the National Front before becoming a Socialist

John Thaw (as Jack Regan in *The Sweeney*)

'Get your trousers on – you're nicked.' (Catchphrase from the TV series)

Phonetically: *Gettch-ore trazzerson – yooor NICK'd.*

Pronunciation tip: Gruff – as befits a man who chain-smokes and drinks copious quantities of whisky. The accent is a cross between Manchester and London. Keep your teeth almost gritted and produce the sound from the back of your throat. For added effect, you could get a mate to 'do' his sidekick, Sergeant George Carter, saying, 'Don't guv, he's not worth it!'

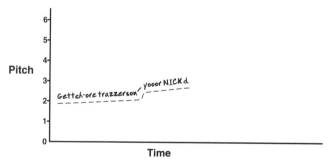

Did you know that John Thaw…?

● was a porter in Manchester's fruit market ● was a CBE ● was once Sir Laurence Olivier's understudy

James Stewart

'If I had my career over again? Maybe I'd say to myself, speed it up a little.' (Quote)

Phonetically: *E-e-e-ff-aye h-h-h-add maye corr-eeer overrr-aggen? Mayyy-beeey-ide s-s-saye term iii-sellff, s-s-speed-ett-upp-a-litt-all.*

Pronunciation tip: You know how some people are described as 'inimitable'? Well, Jimmy Stewart was the complete opposite: completely imitable. He was incomparable, but that's a different thing. So just drawl – nice and slow – and maybe employ a random stutter, always in a different place.

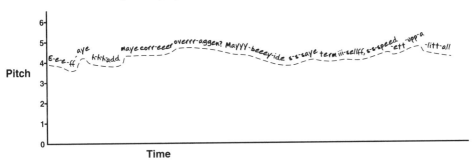

Did you know that James Stewart...?

● saw active service in World War II as a pilot in the US Air Force with the rank of Colonel ● proposed to Olivia de Havilland but she turned him down ● shared a flat with Henry Fonda ● wore a wig

Gene Hackman (as Popeye Doyle in *The French Connection*)

'All right, Popeye's here!' (Line from the film)

Phonetically: *Awe-raitt, popp-ayez-eer!*

Pronunciation tip: Standard New York cop – but with greater vigour, humour and just a little James Stewart-style drawl. Keep your mouth open and force air outwards through your nostrils. Also – for advanced impressions only – don't forget to ask people if they pick their feet in Poughkeepsie.

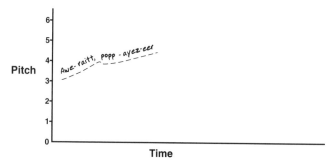

Did you know that Gene Hackman…?

● qualified as a pilot ● shared a flat with Dustin Hoffman and Robert Duvall ● trained as a commercial artist ● has the middle name Alden

Stephen Fry

'I don't watch television: I think it destroys the art of talking about oneself.' (Quote)

Phonetically: *Eye doantt wotch tell-a-vissyan – eye thienkket destroys theeyartoff torlkingg abowet wannselff.*

Pronunciation tip: Posh but not too much. Keep it sonorous with plenty of nose, chest and belly. Fry can be quite epigrammatic in a Wildean sort of way but he doesn't overdo the camp and nor should you.

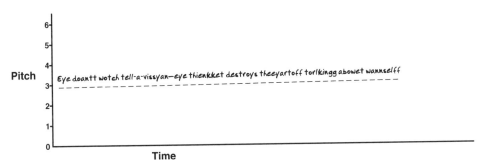

Did you know that Stephen Fry...?

● bought a London cab for his own use ● spent three months in a young offender's institution in 1975 for stealing credit cards ● suffered such bad stage fright in *Cell Mates* (as well as other problems) that he left the country ● was Rowan Atkinson's best man ● chose a suicide pill as his luxury on *Desert Island Discs*

Gerard Depardieu

'I'm happy with very little on this earth, but I do like to have a lot in my glass.' (Quote)

Phonetically: *Ayeem appp-ee weev vey leetle on zees errz, bott ai doo lack towava-lott een mah glasss.*

Pronunciation tip: Inflate your cheeks and give it plenty of top lip – as you would do with any Gallic accent.

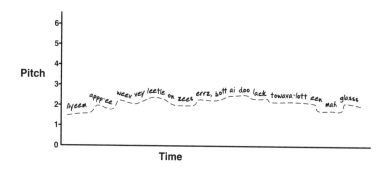

Did you know that Gerard Depardieu...?

● has a photographic memory ● owns a vineyard ● has a tattoo of a star on his arm ● is a keen sculptor

Dick van Dyke (as Bert the 'Cockney' chimney sweep in *Mary Poppins*)

'It's a lovely holiday with Mary.' (Line from the film)

Phonetically: *Yit-ser luvvally ollyday wiv Mare-eee.*

Pronunciation tip: Imagine the worst, most hackneyed Cockney accent and…you're a tenth of the way towards beginning to get there.

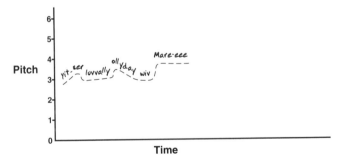

Did you know that Dick van Dyke…?

● is ambidextrous ● was an alcoholic ● his father in *Chitty Chitty Bang Bang* was played by Lionel Jeffries – who's actually younger than him in real life! ● served in the US Air Force

Clive Dunn (as Corporal Jones in *Dad's Army*)

'Don't panic!' (Catchphrase)

Phonetically: *DOANT PANICK!*

Pronunciation tip: Shout it as though you were trying to let the sound escape from the back of your throat. Besides that, just pretend to be a fifty-something man pretending to be an eighty-something man by being simultaneously shrill and frail.

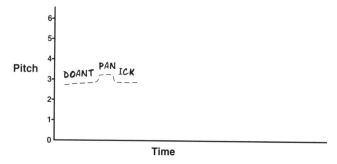

Did you know that Clive Dunn...?

● was in a German POW camp during World War II ● chose his own record on *Desert Island Discs* (*Grandad*) ● the actress Gretchen Franklin is his cousin ● retired to Portugal

Felicity Kendal (as Barbara Good in *The Good Life*)

'Oh Tom, I miss you!' (Line from the show)

Phonetically: *Owe tchom, eyee MISS youu!*

Pronunciation tip: Note that when she says Tom she seems to add a 'ch'. Yup, that's how gorgeous she was. So just think sweet and lovely and 'ickle (like Miss Kendal herself). Unless, of course, you're a bloke (in which case you should be thoroughly ashamed of yourself).

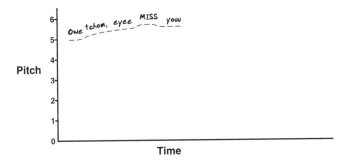

Did you know that Felicity Kendal…?

● was given the childhood nickname Fatty Foo ● had a rose named after her ● chose perfume as her luxury on *Desert Island Discs* ● converted to Judaism ● won the 1981 Rear of the Year award

Marlon Brando (as Terry Malloy in *On The Waterfront*)

'I could have been a contender.' (Line from the film)

Phonetically: *Eye coudda binna contendah.*

Pronunciation tip: Plaintively using your hand for emphasis, speak as though you've got a mouth full of candy-floss. It's worth going online to find the rest of the speech ('it was you, Charlie…'). Great stuff.

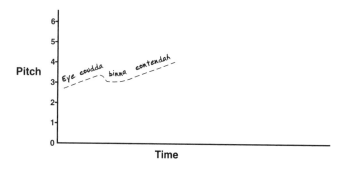

Did you know that Marlon Brando…?
● had alcoholic parents ● had the occupation 'shepherd' on his passport ● was on the cover of *Sgt. Pepper's Lonely Hearts Club Band* ● bought the island of Tetiaroa

Robert De Niro (as Travis Bickle in *Taxi Driver*)

'You talkin' to me?' (Line from the film)

Phonetically: *A-Yew tawkin t'me?*

Pronunciation tip: Tilt your head menacingly while looking in the mirror. Think De Niro imitating Brando in *The Wild One*.

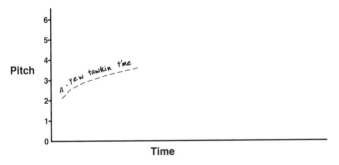

Did you know that Robert De Niro...?

● was given the childhood nickname 'Bobby Milk', because he was so white ● was once served by Richard Gere, who was working as a restaurant waiter before finding fame ● totally ad-libbed the above scene. The script just says, 'Travis looks in the mirror' ● was featured on a Gambian stamp

Vinnie Jones

'All right, son: roll them guns up, count the money, and put your seat belt on.' (Line from *Lock, Stock and Two Smoking Barrels*)

Phonetically: *Auhl-RHYE, Suhn: Ruawl them gahns up, cown-tha muh-nee, an p' ya see' behwls-on.*

Pronunciation tip: Think typical Guy Ritchie all-purpose Cockney/Mockney/Sarf London lairy geezer.

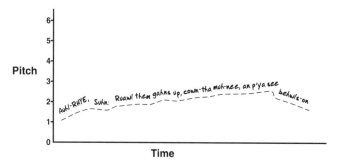

Did you know that Vinnie Jones…?

● has the tattoo 'Leeds Utd' on his leg ● was booked and sent off many times in his career as a professional footballer – including one booking just three seconds into a match ● was banned from flying on Virgin Atlantic after a fight on a flight to Tokyo

Sir Michael Caine

'You were only supposed to blow the bloody doors off!' (Line from *The Italian Job*)

Phonetically: *Yoo wah oooahnly sappooooahs-ta blaow the BLADD-ee daaaw-soff!*

Pronunciation tip: This is an example of Sir Michael's classic Cockney accent, as opposed to his – surprisingly accurate – posh voice. Although this isn't how he achieves the effect, you should keep your lower jaw as immobile as possible and speak as though you were thinking about eating an extremely hot baked potato.

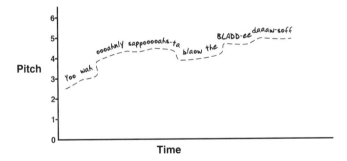

Did you know that Michael Caine…?

● was born Maurice Micklewhite ● as a child had his ears pasted to his head to stop them sticking out
● fought in the Korean War ● had liposuction from his stomach

Joe Pesci (as Tommy DeVito in *Goodfellas*)

'I amuse you? I make you laugh, I'm here to fuckin' amuse you?' (Line from the film)

Phonetically: *Eye a-MEWS yoo? Eye may-kew LAHF, Eyem hir d'fuckin a-MEWS yoo?*

Pronunciation tip: Speak as menacingly as possible. Think an Italian James Cagney.

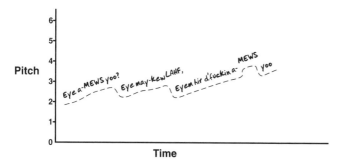

Did you know that Joe Pesci...?

● has eyes of different colours ● co-owns a restaurant with Whoopi Goldberg and Steven Seagal called Eclipse in West Hollywood ● is a keen golfer ● used to sing with the band Joey D and The Starliters

Ray Winstone (as Carlin in *Scum*)

'Right, Banks, you bastard! I'm the daddy now.' (Line from the film)

Phonetically: *Roy-et Bennks, yoo barsterd! Oi-yem the DAD-deee nah.*

Pronunciation tip: Sarf London with maximum aggression. It helps if you're holding a sock full of billiard balls while you're doing it.

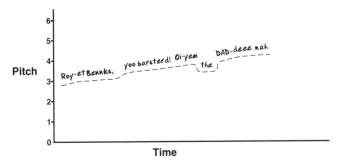

Did you know that Ray Winstone…?
● is a keen horserider ● is a West Ham United fan ● made guest appearances in *Casualty* and *The Bill*

Sir David Jason (as Del Boy in *Only Fools and Horses*)

'Lovely jubbly.' (Catchphrase from the show)

Phonetically: *Lav-lee Jab-lee.*

Pronunciation tip: Peckham, pure Peckham.

Did you know that David Jason…?

- had a twin brother who died at birth, but he didn't discover this until he was 14 • is a keen diver
- 'appeared' in *The Beano* as Del Boy Trotter with Roger the Dodger

John Wayne

'The hell I do.' (Line from *The Shootist* when he's accused of swearing too much)

Phonetically: *Thaaaaa…HELLIDOO.*

Pronunciation tip: Raise your forehead and move your jaw from right to left. Bring your right hand down on the word hell.

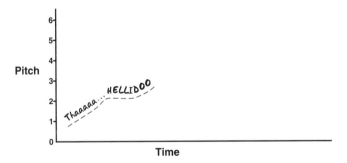

Did you know that John Wayne…?

- won the dog Lassie from its owner in a poker game ● turned down Marlene Dietrich ● was a freemason
- was originally offered Lee Marvin's role in *The Dirty Dozen*

Russell Crowe (as Maximus Decimus Meridius in *Gladiator*)

'At my signal, unleash hell!' (Line from the film)

Phonetically: *Att myy sigg-null, unn-leesh HELLL!*

Pronunciation tip: Since the New Zealand accent is my favourite accent of all, I'd like to use this opportunity to annotate it. Alas, Russell Crowe's accent in *Gladiator* sounds more British (or, rather, Welsh) than Kiwi. To get it right, you're going to have to give it maximum growl and all the authority you can muster. Sadly, this almost certainly won't be enough – especially if you're a woman.

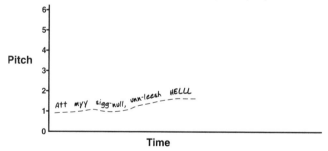

Did you know that Russell Crowe…?

● used to work as a bingo caller ● is the cousin of New Zealand Test cricketers Martin and Jeff Crowe
● is keen on knitting ● had a fear of heights and the sea – both of which he conquered for the film
Master and Commander: The Far Side of the World

Musical People

Dolly Parton

'It takes a lot of money to make a person look this cheap!' (Quote)

Phonetically: *Ett tayeks a lotta munn-ay ta mayek a purr-san look thess cheep!*

Pronunciation tip: Deep South but classy and intelligent with humour. Stick your cheeks out and draw your lips in while maintaining that dazzling smile.

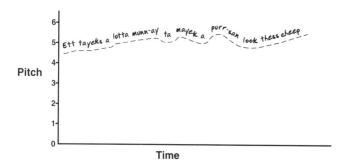

Did you know that Dolly Parton…?

● grew up in poverty ● insured her bust for £2 million ● is one-eighth Cherokee ● was featured on a stamp in Grenada ● sleeps with the light on

Sir Mick Jagger

'I like to look up to women.' (Imagined phrase)

Phonetically: *Oyer loy-ike terrr luck urppp tooooo wimmm-enn.*

Pronunciation tip: You can take the boy out of Dartford but you can't take Dartford out of the boy … or so you'd think. But, in fact, middle-class Mick, the son of teachers, could always talk perfectly well – except when he remembered to establish his 'bad boy' credentials. So to do Mick properly, you're going to have to chew every last syllable (massive lips an advantage) until you have wrung out all the Estuary English you can.

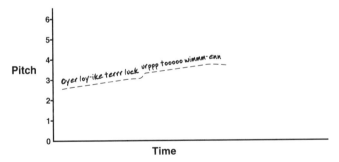

Did you know that Sir Mick Jagger…?

● dropped out of the LSE ● used to work as a hospital porter ● auditioned for the role of Salieri in *Amadeus*. It went to F. Murray Abraham who won the Best Actor Oscar for the role ● was David Bailey's best man

Kylie Minogue

'I don't have to try to be a sex bomb, I am one!' (Quote)

Phonetically: *Aye doawnt hafve ter tri-ter bee ay secks bomm, aye-yam-won!*

Pronunciation tip: Speak as though you're trying to avoid catching your front teeth on your lower lips. Maintain a smile – a genuine one that lights up your eyes, which themselves should stay big as you talk.

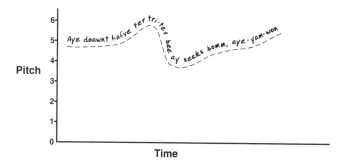

Did you know that Kylie Minogue…?

● is a ballerina's daughter ● was given the childhood nickname Shorty ● is a keen Scrabble player ● made a guest appearance in *The Vicar of Dibley* ● was the inspiration for the Michael Hutchence song *Suicide Blonde*

Rod Stewart

'Instead of getting married again, I'm going to find a woman I don't like and just give her a house.' (Quote)

Phonetically: *Instared uf gettin marrid aggen, aym gonna faind a WOMan eye doan liyek and juss giv-er a howess.*

Pronunciation tip: Imagine you've got a throat full to the brim with gravel. Chain-smoking unfiltered cigarettes is one way to achieve this but gargling with gravel is better for your health.

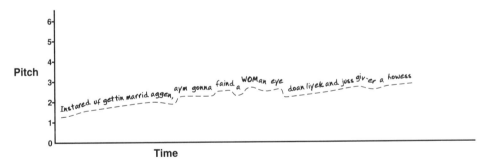

Did you know that Rod Stewart…?

● used to work as a grave digger ● had a trial for Brentford FC ● collects Hornby trainsets ● had a song written about him by Sting (*Peanuts*) ● had his paintings exhibited ● is colour blind

Bruce Springsteen

'Don't call me boss!' (Quote)

Phonetically: *Doan caull me BARSSSS.*

Pronunciation tip: Husky, from the back of the throat – as though you've just been singing for four hours, just like Bruce. Put all your energy into your forehead.

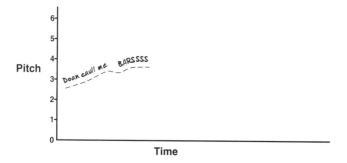

Did you know that Bruce Springsteen…?

● learned to play the guitar by listening to The Rolling Stones' *It's All Over Now* ● sang backing vocals on Lou Reed's *Street Hassle* ● appeared in the film *High Fidelity* ● insured his voice for £3.5 million

Keith Richards

'Cold turkey is not so bad after you've done it ten or twelve times.' (Quote)

Phonetically: *Could turr-kee iz not tso bayd arf-ter yoo-ve dahn-et tenn-ore twell-ve tieyems.*

Pronunciation tip: Do you have any idea what you would have to do to yourself to truly recreate the authentic Keef voice? Please don't, there's only one man in the world who could survive all that he's done and that's the man himself. But, if you want to have a go, it's the same voice as Mick's but a little posher, lispier and – understandably – world-wearier. For some strange reason, there's a trace of seaside landlady in there, too.

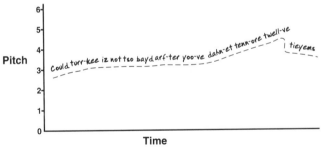

Pitch / Time

Could turr-kee iz not tso bayd arf-ter yoo-ve dahn-et tenn-ore twell-ve tieyems

Did you know that Keith Richards…?

● insured the third finger of his left hand for £1 million ● is the subject of plenty of myths. One is that he has his blood changed regularly. Another is that he, Mick and Marianne were having a foursome with a Mars bar when the police raided his home

Ozzy Osbourne

'Sharon!' (Catchphrase)

Phonetically: *SHA-RUNNN!*

Pronunciation tip: Incredibly, after all those years spent in America and on the road, Ozzy's still got the same Brummie accent he had when he started out. Except now, for understandable reasons, it sounds a bit wasted. So stick with Brummie but, as you speak, think of Bruce Springsteen and Sylvester Stallone in *Rocky* at the top of their emotional range.

Now try these:
'Fuck off!' (Catchphrase)
Phonetically: *Fookk-offff!*

'Of all the things I've lost I miss my mind the most.' (Quote)
Phonetically: *Uv-orll ther things eye-ve losst oye miess moy moynd ther mostt.*

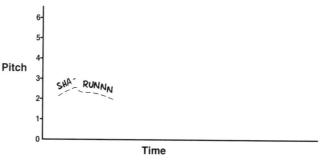

Did you know that Ozzy Osbourne…?

● used to work as a slaughterhouse labourer ● went to jail for burglary. He got two months in 1966
● sleeps with a rifle and a bayonet underneath his bed ● has had a facelift

John Lennon

'We're more popular than Jesus now.' (Quote)

Phonetically: *Ware moor pop-u-ler than JEEEZ-ous nOW.*

Pronunciation tip: Extinct Liverpudlian (fill in your own bad taste gag here) accent that's NOT Scouse. So it's plaintive rather than whiny and just a little posh. Draw the air into your mouth and then exhale it – along with the words – out through your mouth, which shouldn't be too mobile.

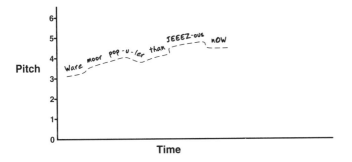

Did you know that John Lennon?
● shoplifted the harmonica he used on *Love Me Do* in Holland ● was an ordained Druid ● used the alias Winston O'Boogie ● had a hotel suite named after him at the Queen Elizabeth Hotel, Montreal

Boy George

'I can do anything. In *GQ*, I appeared as a man.' (Quote)

Phonetically: *Eye cun doo enny-think. In gee-kew-eye app-eered-az-a mann.*

Pronunciation tip: Camp, but not too camp, and stately – with just the odd glottal stop. Mostly throat, rather than tongue and just a little irony, too.

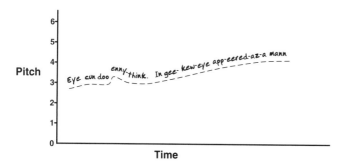

Did you know that Boy George…?

● is a practising Buddhist ● was expelled from Eltham Green School for – according to his headmaster – 'not coming to school and not working' ● made a guest appearance in *The A-Team*

Sir Cliff Richard

'Hi!' (The only word you need to 'do' Cliff!)

Phonetically: *H-eye!*

Pronunciation tip: Before saying anything in a Cliff Richard voice, screw up your nose, lick your lips and bite your bottom lip. Then, when speaking, raise your top lip as high as you can. Use the forefinger of each hand for added emphasis and verisimilitude. Note also: the law of diminishing returns applies to Cliff impressions. Your first in any session of Cliff impressions will always be your best.

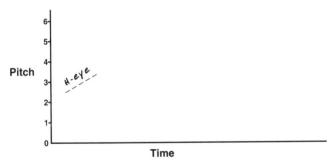

Did you know that Sir Cliff Richard...?

• was born in India with the name Harry Webb • lost his virginity at the age of 18 – with Carol Harris, the wife of Jet Harris of The Shadows • was a Butlin's Redcoat • bought the numberplate MOVE 1T

Eminem

'Sometimes I'm real cool, but sometimes I could be a real asshole.' (Quote)

Phonetically: *Sum-tayimes-ahm reeyal coool butt sum-tayimes ah cood be-ya reeyal ASSSholl.*

Pronunciation tip: Pretend to be a suburban white man trying to sound like an urban black man. Yup, we're in Ali G territory here.

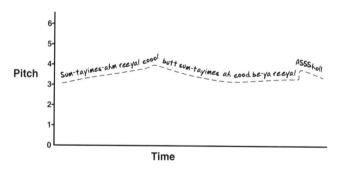

Did you know that Eminem…?

● never knew his father ● originally intended to be a comic-book artist ● has a fear of owls ● has the tattoo 'Slit me' on his wrists. On his stomach is the name of his wife Kim with a tombstone and the inscription 'Rot in Flames' ● remarried his ex-wife

Victoria Beckham

'I haven't read a book in my life.' (Quote)

Phonetically: *Eye hav-unt redda book-inn mye lie-ef.*

Pronunciation tip: She is, of course, a Hertfordshire girl but, hey, don't forget that Herts shares a border with Essex – and so, in a sense, does Victoria's accent. She is, essentially, a posh Essex girl and that's reflected in her slightly sulky voice.

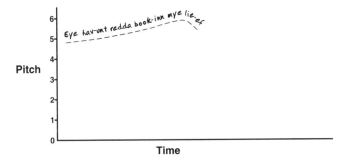

Did you know that Victoria Beckham…?

● had bad adolescent acne ● was bullied at school because of her wealthy background ● was previously engaged to a man called Mark Wood

David Bowie

'David Bowie.'

Phonetically: *Day-VIDD beau-WEEE.*

Pronunciation tip: David Bowie's voice – like Bryan Ferry's – is best conveyed by simply saying – or, rather, singing his name in that unique up-and-down, side-to-side voice.

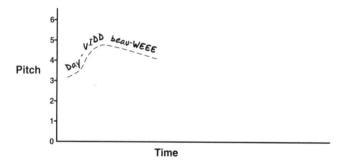

Did you know that David Bowie…?

● was born with the name David Jones ● has eyes of different colours ● trained as a commercial artist ● named his son Zowie (now Joey)

Bono

'Look, I'm sick of Bono and I AM Bono.' (Quote)

Phonetically: *Lurk aoyem sick-ov Bonn-oh eand OY-AM Bonn-oh.*

Pronunciation tip: Soft Dublin accent with a slight wobble which is best achieved by thinking of all the world's problems while you speak.

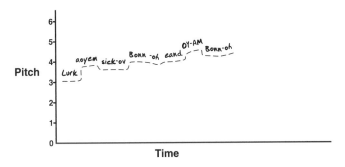

Did you know that Bono…?

● was born with the name Paul Hewson ● was a schoolboy chess champion ● shares a birthday with his daughter Jordan ● named two of his children Memphis Eve and Elijah Bob Patricius Guggi Q

Bob Dylan

'If I wasn't Bob Dylan, I'd probably think that Bob Dylan has a lot of answers myself.' (Quote)

Phonetically: *Eff aye wozz-ent Barb Dill-urn, aye-d prar-bub-lee thienk thurt Barb Dill-urn hazz er-lott-ov ann-serrs muh-seylf.*

Pronunciation tip: These days, His Bobness sounds a lot less like a teenager whose voice has only just broken but he's still hoarse and quietly spoken and mumbles. It's just a lot deeper. Sticking your tongue between your front teeth as you talk should help.

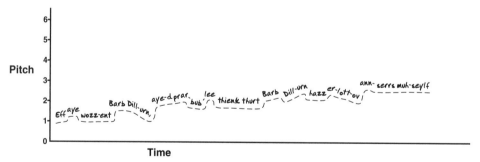

Did you know that Bob Dylan...?

● was a teenage runaway ● wrote the song *Emotionally Yours* for Elizabeth Taylor ● namechecked in the Beatles song *Yer Blues*

Sir Paul McCartney

'I don't take me seriously. If we get some giggles, I don't mind.' (Quote)

Phonetically: *Ai doant taeke mee ser-ee-urse-lee. Effwee get soum gigg-alls ai doant my-ind.*

Pronunciation tip: Move your head around – especially from side to side – as though you were trying to ingratiate yourself with the person you were talking to. Try imagining yourself as a gifted genius who's trying to come across as an ordinary person.

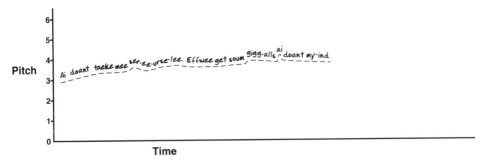

Did you know that Sir Paul McCartney…?

● wrote a children's book called *High in the Clouds: An Urban Furry Tail* ● bought Courtney Love's old house in Los Angeles ● learned to swim as an adult ● wrote the song *We Can Work It Out* for Jane Asher

Ringo Starr

'I'm a mocker.' (Quote. His reply to a reporter who asked him whether he was a mod or a rocker)

Phonetically: *Eye-im-a MOCK-er.*

Pronunciation tip: Ringo's accent hasn't changed much since the Fab Four days – and probably not at all since his impoverished childhood in the Dingle area of Liverpool. (Suburban John was only *pretending* to be a working-class hero: Ringo is the real thing.) So keep it low and flat and, hey presto, you'll turn into Thomas the Tank Engine in front of your friends' eyes.

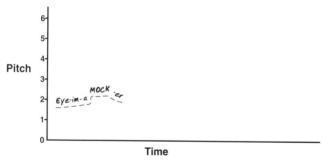

Did you know that Ringo Starr…?

● used to work as a barman ● directed the film *Born To Boogie* (1972) ● is a recovering alcoholic
● has a tattoo of a half-moon on his arm ● had his tonsils removed as an adult

Sting

'Come on, love, just another six hours to go.' (Imagined phrase)

Phonetically: *Cumm-onn lerv jurss an-er-ther sicks–ow-ers ter gerr.*

Pronunciation tip: Soft Geordie accent with just a hint of gravel. Form your mouth into a square shape at the point where the words leave your lips.

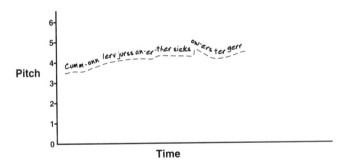

Did you know that Sting…?

● was born with the name Gordon Sumner ● speaks Portuguese ● survived a plane crash ● used to be a school teacher ● his father was a milkman named Ernie

Lulu

'Well…' (The opening word of the song *Shout*)

Phonetically: *WEEEEEEEEEEEEEEEEEEEEEEEEEEEEEEEEEEELLLL*.

Pronunciation tip: This one word helped to shoot the 18-year-old prodigiously talented Lulu straight to stardom. So give it everything you've got – but first make sure the neighbours are out…

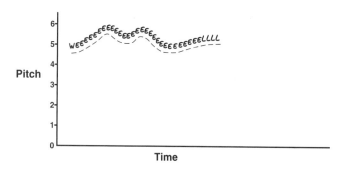

Did you know that Lulu…?

● was born with the name Marie Lawrie ● sang in public for the first time at the age of four ● is a practising Buddhist ● was awarded an honorary doctorate of music by Westminster University

Noel and Liam Gallagher

'You don't speak for the band.' (What Noel said to his brother Liam)

Phonetically: *Yoo dohn' speek fawtha band.*

'You don't speak for the band.' (What Liam said to his brother Noel)

Phonetically: *YOO dohn' speek fawtha band.*

Pronunciation tip: Standard working-class Mancunian – but whinier. Ideally, impersonate Noel when there is someone younger present to impersonate Liam.

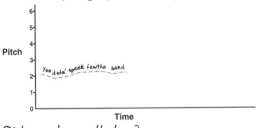

Did you know that...?

- Noel used to be a roadie for The Inspiral Carpets ● Liam got the name Oasis from an Inspiral Carpets poster
- Noel was given the childhood nickname 'Brezhnev' ● Liam was given the childhood nickname 'Weetabix'
- Noel refused to be on *This Is Your Life* ● Liam turned down Paula Yates when she asked him to make love to her in a loo. He told friends, 'She's way too old'

Elvis Presley

'Supersize me.' (Imagined phrase)

Phonetically: *Zerberzize-meah.*

Pronunciation tip: Keep your back teeth closed and move your lips as though you didn't want a deaf person to be able to lip read what you were saying.

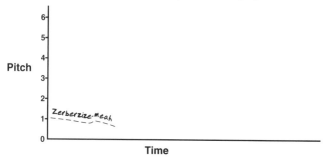

Did you know that Elvis Presley…?

● had a twin brother who died at birth ● once entered an Elvis lookalike contest in a US burger joint and only came third ● started to hip-wiggle out of stage fright. According to Carl Perkins: 'Elvis was so nervous his legs would shake. One day he did it and the crowd went wild. He asked guitarist Scotty Moore, "What'd I do?" and Moore replied, "I don't know but do it again."'

Royals

Queen Elizabeth II

'My husband and I...' (Catchphrase)

Phonetically: *Mye huzbund and-ay...*

Pronunciation tip: Her Maj is a fine woman who does a good job. However, it must be said that her voice is posh and strangulated – although that's probably because we only ever hear her in her official capacity and not when she's talking normally. Don't overdo it or you'll have nothing left for Princes Philip and Charles.

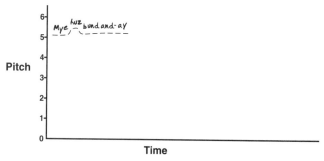

Did you know that Queen Elizabeth II...?

● owns the numberplate HRH 1 ● claimed, with her sister Priness Margaret, that they saw the ghost of Queen Elizabeth I at Windsor Castle when they were girls ● is a gifted impressionist and has done accurate impressions of family members and even politicians

Prince Charles

'Have you come far?' (Catchphrase)

Phonetically: *Havv yoo cumm farr?*

Pronunciation tip: To achieve that unique strangulated sound favoured by so many royals, you have to stretch your lower mouth as far as possible while doing your utmost to keep your teeth clamped together as though you're steeling yourself against an attack of haemorrhoids. This also helps explain why every sentence sounds as though it's preceded by an 'errrr'. If that sounds impossible, then that explains why Charles's accent is so unique.

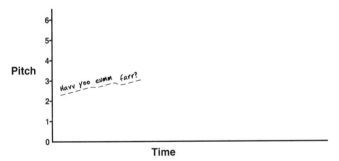

Did you know that Prince Charles…?

● can play the cello ● collects loo seats ● is a proficient magician ● was bullied at school – particularly during rugby games – because he was heir to the throne

Princess Anne

'Naff off.' (Quote)

Phonetically: *Nafff orrff.*

Pronunciation tip: Just like her mother (see earlier) but lower and with total disdain.

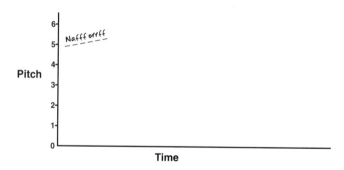

Did you know that Princess Anne…?

● was credited with playing sousaphone on The Bonzo Dog Band's *The Intro and the Outro* ● won the 1971 BBC Sports Personality of the Year Award ● succeeded her maternal grandmother as Chancellor of the University of London ● is the only member of the Royal Family to have participated in the Olympics

Prince Philip

'Dontopedology is the science of opening your mouth and putting your foot in it. I've been practising it for years.' (Quote)

Phonetically: *Don-ter-pedd-oll-ogee iss ther sye-yence of Owe-penning yer maoth end putt-ing your foot-in-ett. H'ayve been prack-tiss-in(g) itt fur yeeers.*

Pronunciation tip: Just like his son, Charles, but with teeth more gritted as though even the act of speaking is distasteful to him. If all else fails, just do Mr Burns from *The Simpsons*. But without the warmth.

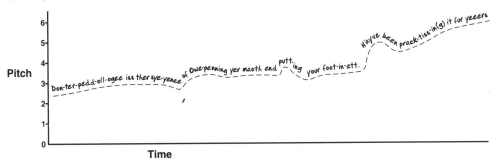

Did you know that Prince Philip…?

● was born on the dining-room table of his parents' house, Mon Repos, in Greece ● was head boy at Gordonstoun school ● was given the childhood nickname Flop ● is fluent in German

TV Presenters

Anne Robinson

'You are the weakest link – goodbye.' (Catchphrase)

Phonetically: *Ewe-ARR the wheek-esst link – GOUD-buy.*

Pronunciation tip: Don't smile, er, obviously, and talk as though you were a prison wardress doing an imitation of a dalek at the precise moment that someone does a loud and smelly fart.

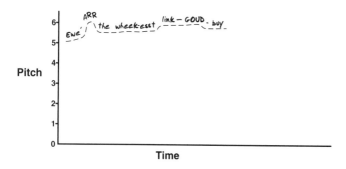

Did you know that Anne Robinson…?

● went to finishing school ● started out as a secretary ● is a recovering alcoholic ● is a gay icon

Sir Trevor Macdonald

'And finally…' (Catchphrase)

Phonetically: *Aeand…fi-nall-ee.*

Pronunciation tip: Trinidadian accent with a cultivated, intelligent tone. Speak with your whole face in a sing-song voice that goes up and down almost at random.

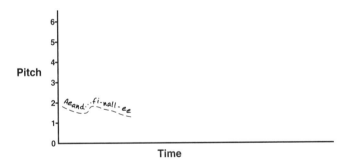

Did you know that Sir Trevor Macdonald…?

● was named George but has always been called Trevor ● was appointed Chancellor of London's South Bank University ● was a Booker Prize judge in 1987

John Humphrys

'Why is this person telling me lies?' (Quote)

Phonetically: *Why-iss this purrs-en tell-ing mee liyes?*

Pronunciation tip: Educated, sonorous Welsh accent. Steely but sing-song and with a touch of gravel.

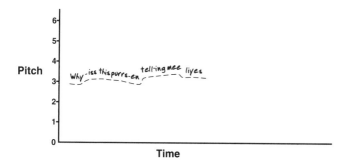

Did you know that John Humphrys…?

● was born in a suburb of Cardiff called Splott ● uses his middle name as a first name – was born Desmond John Humphrys ● is a patron of Pipedown, the campaign against piped music

Carol Vorderman

'You could drastically cut your monthly outgoings with one monthly repayment to First Plus.'
(Line from a TV advertisement in which she appears)

Phonetically: *Yew coud DRAStick-lee CUTT YORE munth-lee OUT-go-ings with WAN munth-lee repayment to FIRST pluss.*

Pronunciation tip: Enunciate your words clearly and deliberately poshly (like a Comprehensive school secretary standing in for the headmistress at assembly) and place the emphasis on words at random.

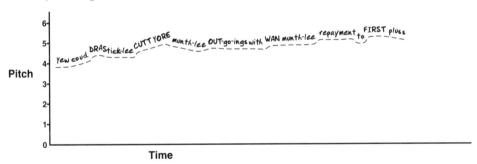

Did you know that Carol Vorderman...?

- has a third-class degree in engineering ● had a fuchsia named after her ('Countdown Carol')
- was a backing singer in the pop group Dawn Chorus and the Blue Tits, fronted by radio DJ, Liz Kershaw

Noel Edmonds

'Deal or no deal.' (Catchphrase)

Phonetically: *Dee-yull ore no dee-yull.*

Pronunciation tip: Classless tone with enough inflection to make him sound like Johnny Vaughan's much less ironic elder brother. The ability to look pleased with yourself and extremely self-assured would be an advantage.

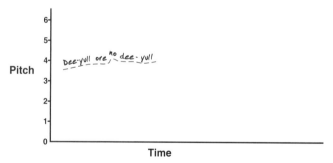

Did you know that Noel Edmonds…?

● attended Brentwood, the same school as Douglas Adams, Keith Allen, Jack Straw and Griff Rhys-Jones
● was appointed Deputy Lieutenant of Devon ● made a guest appearance in *The Detectives* ● chose a motorway service station as his luxury on *Desert Island Discs*

Jeremy Paxman

'Oh, do come on.' (Catchphrase)

Phonetically: *Oh, DOO cumm-onn.*

Pronunciation tip: Try to convey maximum impatience and irritation – combined with a good deal of disbelief. Don't forget to sneer.

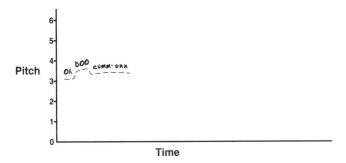

Did you know that Jeremy Paxman...?

● is the father of twins ● made a guest appearance in *The Vicar of Dibley* ● has the middle name Dickson
● lists 'sleeping' as one of his hobbies ● is a keen angler

Ant and Dec

'You're a very funny man, you know.' (Imagined phrase from Ant or Dec to Dec or Ant)

Phonetically: *Yowa verry fonn-ee ma-on, yer know-er.*

'So are you!' (Imagined phrase from Ant or Dec to Dec or Ant)

Phonetically: *Soo arr yooo!*

Pronunciation tip: High-pitched Geordie softened by posh London. Keep smiling – and laughing, as though you were Ant/Dec finding Dec/Ant impossibly funny. Don't forget the Australian-style end-of-phrase inflection.

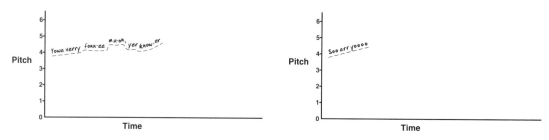

Did you know that Ant and Dec…?

- are keen Scrabble players ● support Newcastle United ● have used the alias Mr Tyne and Mr Wear
- bought houses two doors down from each other in West London's Chiswick

Sir David Frost

'Hello, good evening and welcome.' (Catchphrase)

Phonetically: *HAL-OO, good-eeve-ning andd WELL-comm.*

Pronunciation tip: Keep your mouth open, as though you're about to sneeze but can't quite make it, and narrow your eyes while raising your eyebrows. Then move your bottom teeth from side to side. This may sound like a facial version of Twister but it will produce results.

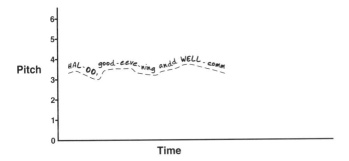

Did you know that Sir David Frost…?

● was a lay preacher ● had a trial for Nottingham Forest FC ● had two previous engagements, to actress Diahann Carroll and to model Karen Graham, but married neither of them

Des Lynam

'Hey, tell you what…' (Catchphrase)

Phonetically: *Hay, tell yoo wott…*

Pronunciation tip: Rich, warm, classless accent with traces of Home Counties and just a tiny Irish lilt. Invest all your charm in this one.

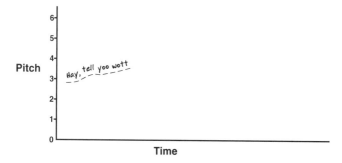

Did you know that Des Lynam…?

● had a Brighton bus named after him ● supports Brighton and Hove Albion ● was a Tie Wearer of the Year

Michael Parkinson

'I have the best job in the world.' (Quote)

Phonetically: *Eye have ther BESSTT job inn ther world.*

Pronunciation tip: If you'll excuse the tautology, Parky's is a gruff Yorkshire accent but with a slight sing-song quality. For greater authenticity, you might want to tug your ear and reminisce about Gene Kelly.

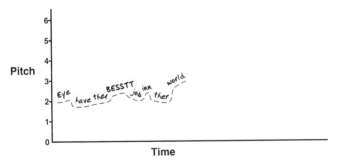

Did you know that Michael Parkinson...?

● was a good enough cricketer to play for Barnsley, along with Dickie Bird and Geoffrey Boycott, and to have a trial for Yorkshire CCC ● appeared as himself in *Brookside* and *Love Actually* ● has had a vasectomy ● took part in Suez when he was, at 19, the youngest Captain in the British Army

Esther Rantzen

'And finally, Cyril...' (Catchphrase from *That's Life*)

Phonetically: *Andd FYE-ner-lee, seer-ull...*

Pronunciation tip: If you listen to her voice long enough, it's actually quite posh – even *grande dame* – but the humour and the warmth redeem it. Bare your teeth as you do the impersonation while thanking your lucky stars that, for you, it's a matter of choice.

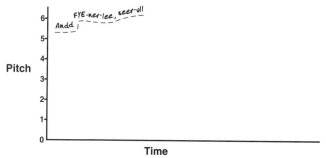

Did you know that Esther Rantzen...?

● lost her virginity at the age of 23 ● switched on the Oxford Street Christmas lights in 1984 ● was awarded an honorary university doctorate by South Bank University

Sir Terry Wogan

'So what do you think of the haircut?' (Imagined phrase)

Phonetically: *Sew whaddya think ov thugh hare-cott?*

Pronunciation tip: Educated, classless Limerick accent. Rich, slightly melodic and with more than a little self-deprecation. Essential that you don't go over the top on the Irish. He doesn't say 'tink' for think or 'der' for the – and nor should you.

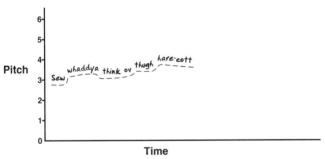

Did you know that Sir Terry Wogan…?

● uses his middle name as a first name. He was born Michael Terry Wogan ● released the single *Floral Dance*
● married his 'childhood sweetheart' and was a virgin on his wedding day ● chose vodka as his luxury on
Desert Island Discs ● has suffered from gout

Joe Pasquale

'Welcome to *The Price is Right*.' (Catchphrase)

Phonetically: *W-well-cum too ther proy-ce-iz royite.*

Pronunciation tip: This one's simple. Just do Frank Spencer from *Some Mothers Do 'Ave 'Em*, the most imitated man in Britain in the 1970s (ask your dad if necessary), one octave higher and two social classes lower. Oh, and just a teensy bit less camp and more strangulated.

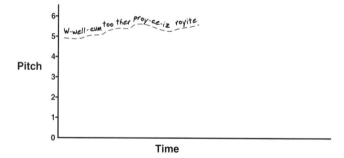

Did you know that Joe Pasquale…?

● left school at 15 ● used to work at Smithfield meat market ● appeared in the 2005 film *Dead Long Enough*
● was the only British comedian to star in The Muppets 25th Anniversary show

Jeremy Clarkson

'We all know that small cars are good for us. But so is cod liver oil. And jogging.' (Quote)

Phonetically: *Wee awl noo thert smawll karss-arr goodd fer-uss. Butt sew-iz codd livv-er-oyl. Andd JOGG-ing.*

Pronunciation tip: Jeremy Clarkson's is the voice of our age – which is why almost every other male broadcaster tries to sound like him. And not just on *Top Gear*. He's funny and smart and ironic – all of which are reflected in his voice. Enunciate your words carefully and keep it deep and gravelly to stop yourself lapsing into Johnny Vaughan.

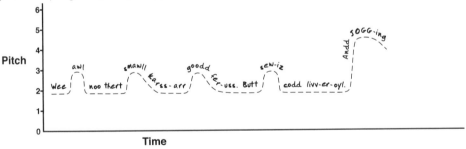

Did you know that Jeremy Clarkson...?

● is the son-in-law of a VC winner ● passed his driving test in his grandfather's Bentley ● was on the very last Concorde flight ● was expelled from Repton for many minor offences which his headmaster compared to being poked in the chest every day – for five years

Murray Walker

'I make no apologies for their absence – I'm sorry they're not here.' (Quote during commentary)

Phonetically: *EYE MAYKE NO APPOLLO-GEES FORE THER-ABB-SENSE – AYIM SORREE THEYER NOTT HEER.*

Pronunciation tip: Best if you almost shout it. It's Alan Partridge at full throttle with plenty of echo and vibrato – but more affable and with back notes of self-deprecation.

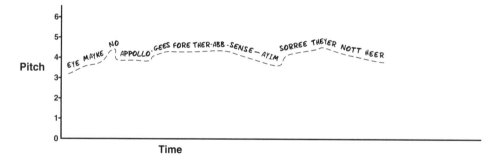

Did you know that Murray Walker…?

● drove a tank in World War II ● had a hip replaced ● had a day job in advertising for most of his commentating career and worked on the 'Mars a Day' campaign

Chris Tarrant

'But we don't want to give you that!' (Catchphrase)

Phonetically: *Bert-wee doant-wan-ter givv ewe THATT!*

Pronunciation tip: An almost perfect mix of Kenneth Clarke and Barry Norman. To 'do' CT, you have to speak with vitality and charm. Force the words off your tongue to the top of your mouth while keeping your cheeks high and your brow furrowed.

Now try these:
'Is that your final answer?' (Catchphrase)
Phonetically: *Iz thaet yore FIE-nal arnserr?*

'Tee hee' (Catchphrase – sorry, Chris)
Phonetically: *Teeee heeee.*

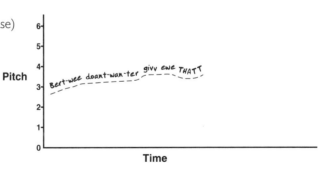

Did you know that Chris Tarrant…?

● lived in his van for six months when he was homeless ● was an only child ● is a keen angler ● used to be an English teacher

Jim Bowen

'You can't beat a bit of bully.' (Catchphrase in *Bullseye*)

Phonetically: *Yercantbeetabitabull-ee.*

Pronunciation tip: Lancashire accent with the words spoken in a torrent, as befits catchphrases, and as though you were pushing air out of your lungs and through your vocal tract in a manner technically described as 'pulmonic egressive'. Now you know.

Now try this:
'Super smashing great'
(Catchphrase in *Bullseye*)
Phonetically: *soopa-smash-ing-grate*

Did you know that Jim Bowen…?
● was born James Whittaker ● bought a Harley-Davidson motorcycle ● is the 'agony uncle' for the University of Central Lancashire's Students' Union newspaper

Paul O'Grady

'When I want your lot's opinion, I'll slap it out of you.' (Line from his act)

Phonetically: *Wenn-aye wont yorre-lotz opin-yan, ayel SerLAPPitzowtov-ewe.*

Pronunciation tip: Whingeing Liverpudlian, pitched high.

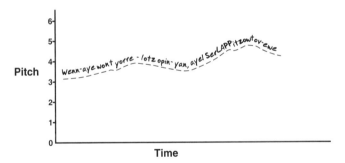

Did you know that Paul O'Grady…?

● used to be a social worker ● bought Vic Reeves's house in Aldington, Kent, which was formerly owned by Sir Noel Coward ● appeared as himself in *Brookside*

Lorraine Kelly

'Och, I'm just a wee thing.' (Imagined phrase)

Phonetically: *Auhkkke, ayim jest-a WEEE theng.*

Pronunciation tip: Thick Scottish with evident desire to charm. Draw your lips together and smile – with your eyes, too – for true authenticity.

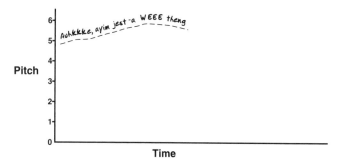

Did you know that Lorraine Kelly...?

● has run the London marathon ● is a gay icon ● is a big *Star Trek* fan ● was a girl guide

Cilla Black

'Lot of lot of laughs.' (Catchphrase)

Phonetically: *Lorra lorra larffs.*

Pronunciation tip: Slightly whiny Scouse accent (forgive the tautology). Say it as though you might break down (in tears or in laughs) at any moment.

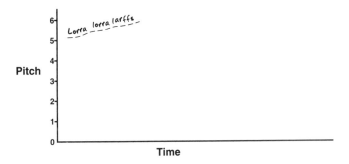

Did you know that Cilla Black…?

● chose *Anyone Who Had a Heart*, one of her own records, on *Desert Island Discs* ● started out as a secretary ● had a nose job ● had her eyesight corrected by laser surgery

Johnny Vaughan

'How about that, gang?' (Quote)

Phonetically: Howw-er-boutt-THATT gang?

Pronunciation tip: The ultimate lad, with a genuinely classless accent – which is what you get when you spend time in public school and then in prison. The key to doing Johnny is to make it all ironic (and post-modern) without ever being sardonic. In other words, keep it fun and if you can hear his voice in your inner ear, then you can't fail to get it right.

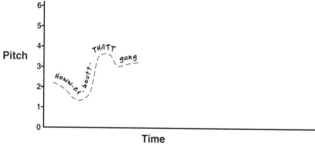

Did you know that Johnny Vaughan...?

● was born at the precise time that Bobby Charlton scored for England against Mexico in the 1966 World Cup ● has worked as a grill chef, jewel courier, sales assistant and video shop manager ● became a Catholic ● went to jail for drugs – four years in 1988 ● is an honorary Butlin's Redcoat

Sportsmen

David Beckham

'Coming, darling – I'm just in the loos.' (Imagined phrase)

Phonetically: *Cumm-ingg dar-link – eyem jusstin ther looz.*

Pronunciation tip: Weedy and thin, unlike the lad himself. Imagine Norman Wisdom at the same age, just after he's been run down by a bus, and you should be almost there.

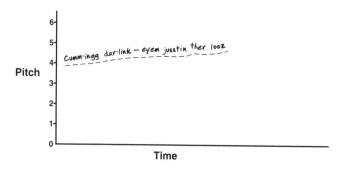

Did you know that David Beckham…?

● is good at DIY ● salutes magpies ● is a gay icon ● is teetotal

Paul Gascoigne

'I never make predictions, and I never will.' (Quote)

Phonetically: *Ah nivver mekk predd-ick-shuns and-ah nivver wi-lle.*

Pronunciation tip: Standard Geordie – with tears for added accuracy. Remember to raise your voice at the end of the sentence.

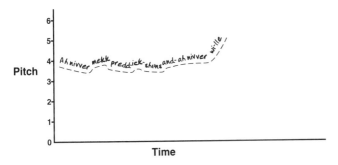

Did you know that Paul Gascoigne...?

● has suffered from Obsessive Compulsive Disorder (OCD) ● is a member of the Dennis the Menace Fan Club ● was named after Paul McCartney ● is a keen angler

Darren Gough

'Would you like the next dance?' (Imagined phrase)

Phonetically: *Wood-ya liyek tha necks-danss?*

Pronunciation tip: Yorkshire – but not too flat or too rounded – and with warmth, humour and liveliness.

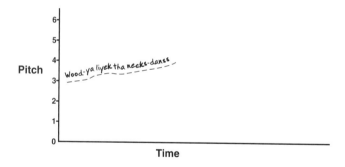

Did you know that Darren Gough...?

● supports Tottenham Hotspur ● won the second series of *Strictly Come Dancing* ● is England's eighth most successful bowler ● is new rhyming slang for 'cough'

Arsène Wenger

'You cannot say that you are happy when you don't win.' (Quote)

Phonetically: *Yooo kenn-otte say zhat yoow-are app-ee when yooo don-tt ween.*

Pronunciation tip: French accent – obviously – with just a touch of German. No need to smile. Just keep your mouth pursed and shrug your shoulders.

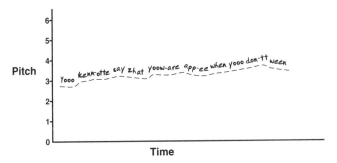

Did you know that Arsène Wenger…?
● holds a master's degree in economics from the University of Strasbourg ● is nicknamed 'The Professor' ● is Arsenal's most successful manager in terms of the number of trophies won ● was awarded the Legion d'Honneur, France's highest decoration, in 2002 and an honorary OBE the following year

Wayne Rooney

'So what did you buy today, Colleen?' (Imagined phrase)

Phonetically: *Sir wott did-yer buy-ee terdaye, Coll-eeen?*

Pronunciation tip: Standard Scouse, but you'll need to pull your face into the shape of a potato to get it quite right.

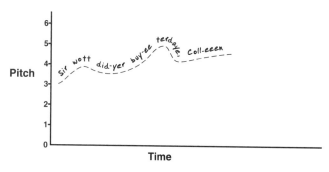

Did you know that Wayne Rooney…?

● is the son of a boxer and is descended from the heavyweight boxing champion, Bob Fitzsimmons
● named his pet Chow-Chow Fizz ● has his girlfriend Colleen's name tattooed onto his shoulder

Frankie Dettori

'Out of the way – I'm about to do a flying dismount!' (Imagined phrase)

Phonetically: *Atta tha waya – ahma batt tadawa flayin dissmoun!*

Pronunciation tip: If I say 'do a cartoon Italian accent', don't blame me – just blame Frankie!

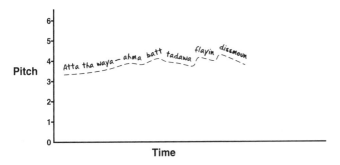

Did you know that Frankie Dettori…?
● supports Arsenal ● was a team captain on TV's *A Question of Sport* ● survived a plane crash
● presented *Top of the Pops*

Thierry Henry

'Va va voom.' (Phrase he uses in the ads for Renault Clio)

Phonetically: *Va-va voooom.*

Pronunciation tip: Very cool French accent with plenty of puffed cheek and shrugged shoulders.

Now try this:
'Sometimes in football you have to score goals.' (Quote)
Phonetically: *Somme-tie-ems-in-foote-bal yoo haff too scorre gollz.*

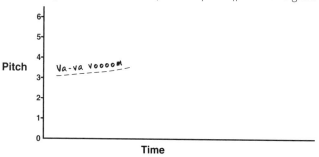

Did you know that Thierry Henry…?

● is 6' 2" tall ● has a father from Guadeloupe and a mother from Martinique ● is the only player ever to win the European Golden Boot for two seasons in succession ● is Arsenal's all-time greatest goalscorer

Sir Alex Ferguson

'The lads ran their socks into the ground.' (Quote)

Phonetically: *Tha ludz rann thayre sorcks-intae tha grouw'nd.*

Pronunciation tip: Sir Alex has never lost his Govan accent so you should give it the full Glaz-gee treatment, stopping just short of adding 'see you, Jimmy' at the end of every sentence.

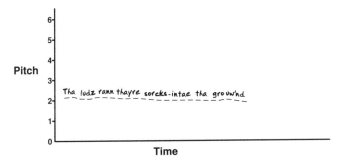

Did you know that Sir Alex Ferguson…?

● has cited *Treasure Island* by Robert Louis Stevenson as his favourite children's book ● is a keen snooker player ● has a heart pacemaker ● was awarded an honorary university doctorate by Robert Gordon University in Aberdeen

Phil Tufnell

'You can't smoke twenty a day and bowl fast.' (Quote)

Phonetically: *Yer carnt smow-ke twenny-er-day andd bow(a)ll forst.*

Pronunciation tip: Mockney, Mockney, Mockney. Think geezer, speak geezer, be geezer.

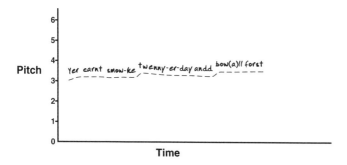

Did you know that Phil Tufnell…?

● has a strong dislike of flying ● has the middle names Clive and Roderick ● is 6' 2" tall ● was given the nickname 'Cat' – not because of his agility as a cricketer but because he liked to take catnaps

John McEnroe

'You cannot be serious!' (Quote)

Phonetically: *EWE KERN NARTT BEE SEER-EE-YUS!*

Pronunciation tip: Think young American in absolute torment, even though it was a dodgy line-call in a game of tennis. Hold nothing back. He didn't.

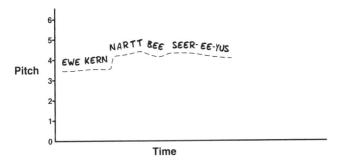

Did you know that John McEnroe...?

● 'phoned up' Frasier in an episode of the hit comedy ● was married to Ryan O'Neal's daughter, Tatum ● was featured on a stamp in Sierra Leone ● was born in Germany

Sven Goran Eriksson

'I think we played rather well.' (Quote)

Phonetically: *Eye thenk wee plaid rar-thher welll.*

Pronunciation tip: Contemplative, considered and well spoken, there's a melodic element to Sven's voice but only within a very limited range, thereby ensuring that the overall effect isn't too exciting.

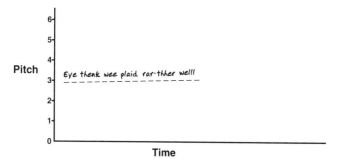

Did you know that Sven Goran Eriksson...?

● was awarded the King's Medal, the second highest honour a Swedish commoner can get, in 2006, for his contribution to sport ● had to retire from playing football at the age of 27 due to a knee injury

Pelé

'A penalty is a cowardly way to score.' (Quote)

Phonetically: *Uh penn-al-tee ees-a cow-ad-lee-way too scorr.*

Pronunciation tip: Talk with poise, dignity and confidence. For maximum effect, imagine you've just gargled with clear honey.

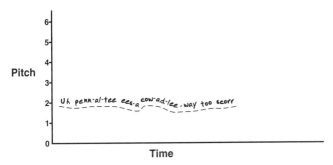

Did you know that Pelé ...?

● has the real name Edson Arantes do Nascimento, and was named after Thomas Edison ● grew up in poverty ● was the cause of a 48-hour ceasefire when, in 1970, the two factions involved in a civil war in Nigeria agreed to halt hostilities in order to watch Pelé play an exhibition game in Lagos ● is the father of twins

Boris Becker

'Where's the broom cupboard?' (Imagined phrase)

Phonetically: *Vairz ze brOOm cubbudd?*

Pronunciation tip: Standard German with a slight lisp.

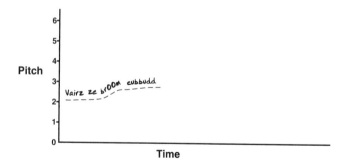

Did you know that Boris Becker…?

● is the son of an architect ● was convicted of tax evasion in 2002 in Germany. He avoided jail but was fined and given two years' probation ● was the youngest Wimbledon winner, aged 17 ● is a keen chess player

Politicians

Tony Blair

'I'm a pretty straight sort of guy.' (Quote)

Phonetically: *Eye-ma prett-ee strayte sortta guyy.*

Pronunciation tip: Perhaps the hardest tip in the whole book, as Blair is such a chameleon. Depending on whom he's with, he can be anything – from posh English to Estuary English to Edinburgh Scottish. This quote is taken from what might be called the middle of his range. Think Cliff Richard, his holiday host, without the sincerity.

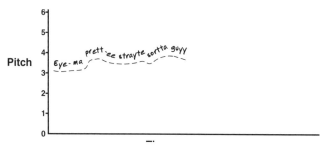

Did you know that Tony Blair...?

● attended the same school as Rowan Atkinson (Durham Choristers Preparatory School) ● played himself on *The Simpsons* ● was the lead singer in the university band, The Ugly Rumours, which also included the broadcaster Mark Ellen

Gordon Brown

'Prudence.' (Catchphrase)

Phonetically: *Prooodunsse.*

Pronunciation tip: Educated Scottish with maximum seriousness. Remember, Gordon can't speak and breathe at the same time and so he breathes – only when he absolutely has to – by opening his mouth like a fish.

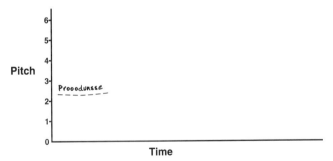

Did you know that Gordon Brown...?

● uses his middle name as a first name – was born James Gordon Brown ● got a first in history from Edinburgh University before becoming the university's rector ● won a *Daily Express* competition for a vision of Britain in the year 2000, when he was just 21 ● doesn't drive

William Hague

'The most expensive haircut I ever had cost ten pounds.' (Quote)

Phonetically: *(Ah) theh MOAST-ex-PENN-siv HHARE-cot (h)ey-evver hhadd cosst ttenn powendss.*

Pronunciation tip: Imagine that Harold Wilson and Enoch Powell had a love child. Not a pleasant thought, I accept, but the result if it had been a male would have sounded spookily like William Hague.

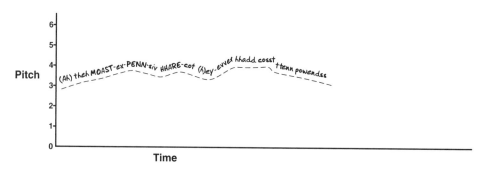

Did you know that William Hague…?

● shared a flat with Alan Duncan ● is colour blind ● is a keen judoist ● like Bill Clinton, has the forenames William Jefferson

Tony Benn

'It's all a media conspiracy.' (Imagined phrase)

Phonetically: *Itssh-awl-er meejah consh-pier-ashy.*

Pronunciation tip: Doubtless, he'll claim that this is another media (meejah) conspiracy but he does (doesh) have a slight lisp, which causes him to chew his words (wordsh) as he speaks (speaksh). Use your hands, but not your arms, to emphasise your points.

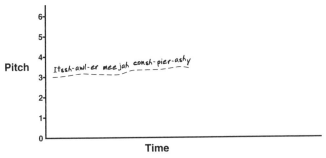

Did you know that Tony Benn...?

● joined the RAF in 1943 at the age of 18 and and got his wings just as Germany surrendered, and so he switched to the Fleet Air Arm to fight against Japan ● was 'baby' of the House of Commons, when he was elected at the age of 25 in 1950 ● chose *Das Kapital* by Karl Marx as his book on *Desert Island Discs*

Ken Livingstone

'If voting changed anything, they'd abolish it.' (Quote)

Phonetically: *Iff voat-ing chayng-d enny-thing, thayd-erboll-ishit.*

Pronunciation tip: His accent is a mixture of South London and Estuary English. Use your lips sparingly and let your words come out through your nose at the same time as they emerge from your mouth.

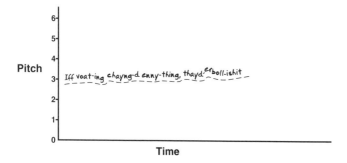

Did you know that Ken Livingstone…?
● used to be a cancer research technician ● failed the 11+ exam ● doesn't drive

President George W. Bush

'Those who enter the country illegally violate the law.' (Quote)

Phonetically: *Tho-ze hoo enn-turr ther kerntree illee-gerlee vye-OWE-late ther laww.*

Pronunciation tip: What can I say – except that he's the only entry in the whole book who you'll get right by doing it wrong.

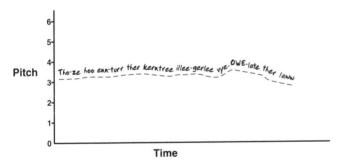

Did you know that President George W. Bush…?

● collects autographed baseballs ● has run a marathon ● is teetotal ● speaks Spanish

Ann Widdecombe

'Don't interrupt me.' (Quote)

Phonetically: *DOANTT interr-UPTT mee.*

Pronunciation tip: Like a lad whose voice is breaking, her voice is all over the place. It goes unexpectedly high and then comes down again. Use your front teeth to clip the words as they come out.

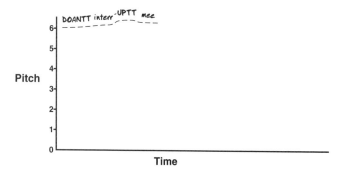

Did you know that Ann Widdecombe…?

- has a fear of heights ● failed the 11+ exam after developing whooping cough with complications
- came in at number 94 in the 2003 poll of the 100 Worst Britons ● was a convent schoolgirl

Baroness Margaret Thatcher

'The lady's not for turning.' (Quote)

Phonetically: *The lay-deez nott forr turr-ning.*

Pronunciation tip: One minute patronising (with a deeper voice), the next browbeating (in a higher voice). Subtle weak 'r', which her daughter has inherited big time.

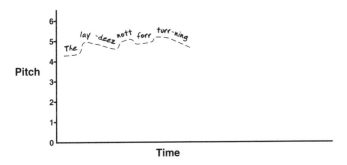

Did you know that Baroness Margaret Thatcher...?
● was head girl at Kesteven and Grantham Girls' School ● has a fear of the dark ● was a research chemist before qualifying as a barrister ● suffers from insomnia ● had a rose named after her

Bill Clinton

'I did not have sex with that woman.' (Quote)

Phonetically: *Ah di'nod hay'ev say'ex with tha' woum-en.*

Pronunciation tip: Think good ol' boy lying as though his life depended on it, which, of course, it did. Look directly at whomever you're talking to. Don't look away and don't blink.

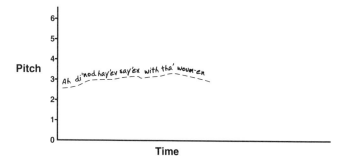

Did you know that Bill Clinton…?

● collects saxophones, both real ones and miniatures ● has a photographic memory ● never knew his father ● is allergic to flowers ● is hard of hearing

...And Anyone Else Who Knows Me

Jordan

'Can you tell me what my toes look like?' (Imagined phrase)

Phonetically: *Kenn ya tewell me waugh mah tAOSe look loiyak?*

Pronunciation tip: Elongate your face and keep your lips as far apart as possible (insert own punchline here). Keep it expressionless.

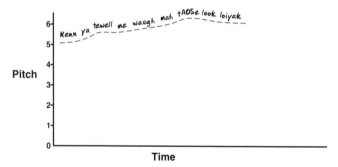

Did you know that Jordan...?

- is keen on sewing ● says *I Should Be So Lucky* by Kylie was the first record she ever bought
- was ranked second in a list of the '100 Worst Britons We Love to Hate' on Channel 4 (2003)
- was runner-up in a survey to find Britain's top fantasy cab companion

Michael Winner

'Haven't you got anything more expensive?' (Imagined phrase)

Phonetically: *Heaven't yew gott ENNYtheng moor exspensieve?*

Pronunciation tip: Try doing an upper-class version of Alec Guinness's Fagin from the 1948 version of *Oliver Twist*. Author's note: writing as someone who is himself Jewish, it is impossible to overdo the stock Jewish character beloved of anti-Semites everywhere, so don't worry, my dear, and just go for it.

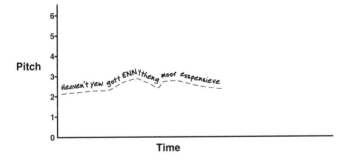

Did you know that Michael Winner...?

● confessed to having shoplifted in his youth: 'I stole from shops and from pupils at school' ● has never married ● was Marco Pierre White's best man

Uri Geller

'The spoon is bending!' (Quote)

Phonetically: *Ther spoon iss BENN-ding!*

Pronunciation tip: Think of Woody Allen with an Israeli accent. So it's very whiny but – unlike Woody – there's not a lot of irony or humour. Sound as though you're amazed at your own incredible powers.

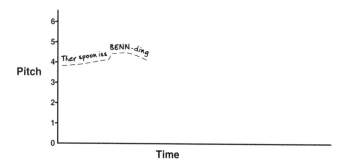

Did you know that Uri Geller…?

● used to live on a kibbutz ● was bulimic ● had Michael Jackson as his best man when he renewed his marriage vows ● released a solo album (*Uri Geller*, 1975) ● served in the Israeli army

Jerry Hall

'To be a good wife, you've got to be a maid in the house, a cook in the kitchen and a whore in the bedroom.' (Quote)

Phonetically: *Ter bee-ya gerdd why-iff, yo-ve gart-ter bee-ya may-id in ther hayouse, er kerk in ther kitt-chin aynd-er hooor in ther bedd-rerm.*

Pronunciation tip: Sexy Texan drawl. Impossible to overdo so long as you smile as you speak.

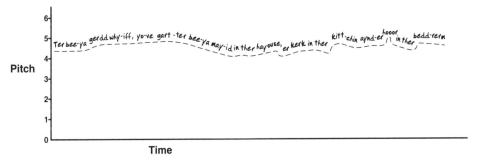

Did you know that Jerry Hall…?

● is the daughter of a truck driver ● lost her virginity at the age of 15 to a rodeo rider – who kept his boots on ● was engaged to Bryan Ferry, and the joke goes that Mick Jagger 'rescued' her from becoming Jerry Ferry

Yoko Ono

'John and I were like one person.' (Quote)

Phonetically: *Joh ann-ai waa layi(k) wah purrso.*

Pronunciation tip: Combination of American and Japanese. Mostly high in the voice and breathy and don't pronounce the consonants.

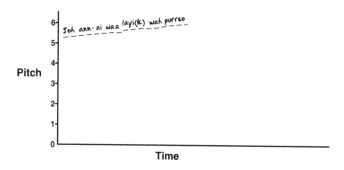

Did you know that Yoko Ono...?

● is a vegetarian ● appeared in the film *Satan's Bed* ● has been the butt of plenty of jokes, but none finer than a quip by Joan Rivers, who said, 'If I found her floating in my pool, I'd punish my dog.' Think about it.

Nigella Lawson

'I don't believe in low-fat cooking.' (Quote)

Phonetically: *Aye doane-t bee-leeve inn lowe-fatt cook-ing.*

Pronunciation tip: A cross between the Queen and Anna Ford. In other words, very, very posh – think 'Mrs Cholmondley-Warner shows you how to eat'.

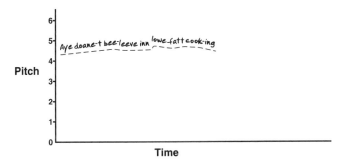

Did you know that Nigella Lawson...?

- attended the same school as Samantha Bond and Davina McCall (Godolphin and Latymer in West London)
- failed her 11+ for refusing to take a maths paper ● came in at number 90 in the 2003 poll of the 100 Worst Britons

Gordon Ramsay

'Come here, you.' (Quote)

Phonetically: *Cameer YEEW.*

Pronunciation tip: Posh Glaswegian with swear words added (to taste).

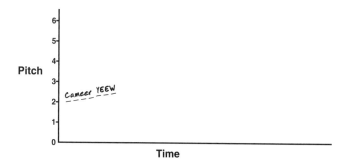

Did you know that Gordon Ramsay...?

● was a professional footballer who played two games for Rangers ● left school at 15 ● is the father of twins ● has run the London marathon several times

Jamie Oliver

'Pukka.' (Catchphrase)

Phonetically: *PUCK-ERR.*

Pronunciation tip: As he's grown older and more successful, he's had the confidence to ditch – or at least modify – that dreadful cheeky chappie Mockney accent. The result is that he now sounds like a perfectly normal human being. The lisp, however, remains.

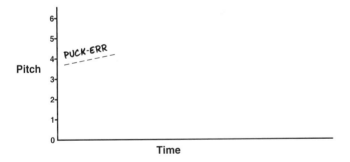

Did you know that Jamie Oliver...?

● was cooking in his father's pub at the age of eight ● married his 'childhood sweetheart' ● used to be a drummer in a band called Scarlet Division ● is dyslexic

Clive James

'I've got a monumental conceit.' (Quote)

Phonetically: *Ayve gott er MONN-U-MENTAL conn-seet.*

Pronunciation tip: Move your upper mouth up so high that your eyes narrow. Keep your lips open at all times but don't move them very much.

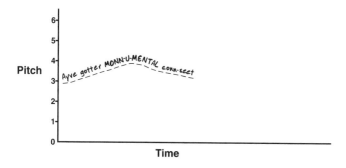

Did you know that Clive James...?

● worked as a lion-cage cleaner ● appeared on *University Challenge* as a competitor ● acted in *Neighbours* ● can speak Japanese ● chose Space Invaders as his luxury on *Desert Island Discs*

Sharon Osbourne

'If anybody says their facelift doesn't hurt, they're lying.' (Quote)

Phonetically: *If fenny-bod-ee sez there fayceliftt dozent hurt, there lie-ying.*

Pronunciation tip: Upwardly mobile North London dumped somewhere in the middle of the Atlantic. I think that if you could create a hybrid of the voices of Maureen Lipman, David 'Kid' Jensen and Joe Pasquale then you would get Sharon Osbourne. But how to prove it? So talk confidently and deliberately – or as confidently and deliberately as all that cosmetic surgery will allow.

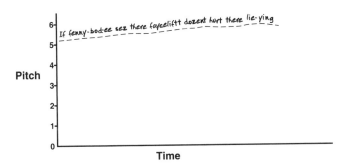

Did you know that Sharon Osbourne...?

● met Ozzy when she was 17 ● married Ozzy in Hawaii in 1982 ● briefly managed the group, Queen

Tara Palmer-Tomkinson

'Have I done something silly?' (Imagined phrase)

Phonetically: *Haff-eye dunn sum-thingk sill-ee?*

Pronunciation tip: Sexy, breathy, slightly clipped and just a tiny bit lazy in tone. Combination of Felicity Kendal and, for the benefit of older readers, Fenella Fielding.

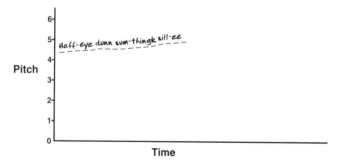

Did you know that Tara Palmer Tomkinson…?

● is the daughter of Charles, who represented Great Britain at skiing in the 1964 Winter Olympics
● is a fine pianist ● allegedly replied to Sir James Goldsmith, when he told her he planned to launch a new political party in the UK: 'Which party is that? I think I'm supposed to be going.' ● writes poetry

Sir Alan Sugar

'You're fired!' (His catchphrase in *The Apprentice*)

Phonetically: *Yaw FIE-yerd!*

Pronunciation tip: Hackney accent – with added upward mobility. Jab your finger as you deliver the first syllable of 'fired'.

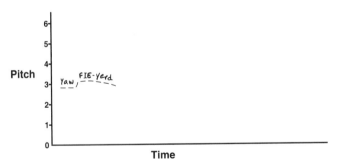

Did you know that Sir Alan Sugar...?

● failed the 11+ exam ● founded Amstrad (Alan Michael Sugar TRADing) ● started off by selling fruit and veg from a van ● used to be Chairman of Tottenham Hotspur

Carol Thatcher

'I'll try anything!' (Imagined phrase)

Phonetically: *Ayill twwy ennee-thing!*

Pronunciation tip: Wonderful Empire woman who should really be called Bunty or something equally suitable. Think gym mistress of a certain age who has enormous trouble with her 'r's but doesn't give a damn so long as there's some fun to be had somewhere. Slightly deeper voice than her mother's.

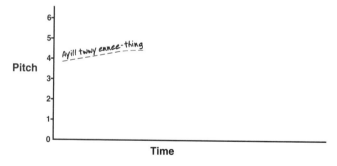

Did you know that Carol Thatcher…?

● had a relationship with Jonathan Aitken ● once walked out of a Billy Connolly gig after he was rude about her mother ● won the fifth series of *I'm a Celebrity…Get Me Out of Here!*